kittens are EVIL II

Little Heresies in Public Policy

kittens
are
EVIL II

Little Heresies in Public Policy

edited by:

Charlotte Pell

Rob Wilson

Toby Lowe

Jan Myers

tp

Triarchy Press

Published in this first edition in 2020 by:

Triarchy Press

Axminster, England

+44 (0)1297 561335

info@triarchypress.net

www.triarchypress.net

A catalogue record for this book is available from the British Library.

ISBNs:

Print: 978-1-911193-77-7

ePub: 978-1-911193-78-4

pdf: 978-1-911193-79-1

Contents

Foreword

by Anton Hemerijck
Professor of Political Science: European University Institute, Florence
Centennial Professor of Social Policy: London School of Economics and
Political Science

John Maynard Keynes is purported to have said "when the facts change, I change my mind!" Surely, if ever there was a lucid, independent, 20th-century mind, it was Keynes's. Most of us harbour a more defensive posture, prone to relegate 'facts change' to exceptions from standard operating procedures in need of governance re-affirmation. As a collective endeavour, policy adaptation to changing realities is even more difficult for two reasons. Public policy is fundamentally geared towards (conflicting) objectives, such as full employment, economic growth, low inflation, more nurses and nurseries, less poverty, subdued inequality, and greenhouse gas reduction – commendable targets that are inherently uncertain. As such, there is an established tendency, however foolish, to re-commit to underlying rules and governance structures in times of need, when policy outputs deviate from aspired targets.

The second conundrum lies in the reality that public policy results from interactions among a multitude of policy actors, each with their own understanding of problems and solutions, and each with their own political preferences and interests. For day-to-day policy makers, unsurprisingly, it's the rule-structure that provides governance leverage and professional security, not political objectives *per se*. On a positive note, this gives policy a requisite element of stability and predictability. On the other hand, we are far removed from the appealing dictum 'when facts change, reform follows suit'.

Change is difficult, but it happens! The example of the experience of the Great Recession in Europe is instructive. Immediately after the 2007-8 crash, many OECD governments showed little inhibition in pursuing bold strategies of crisis management, on a scale unthinkable a decade earlier when market-liberal ideas were cemented into the policy-making machinery of advanced capitalist democracies. At first, crisis management focused on financial sector bailouts. Next, central banks took on new functions, including liquidity and credit enhancing interventions. With some delay, the European Central Bank (ECB), with Mario Draghi at the helm, stepped out of the void to save the euro, doing 'whatever it takes' through bond buying and quantitative easing, far beyond the narrow remit of inflation targeting in the Maastricht Treaty. But here is where the good news ends.

All the heresies in this volume are characterised by an astute readiness to give up on received wisdom, but no less hidden is the ambition, which I share, to one day be accepted as mainstream. Second, all the essays point to problematic mismatches between the substantive design of policy programmes and their institutional governance structures, which continue to rely on by-now outdated policy theories. Third, in recognition of institutional shortcomings, as a way forward, most proposals suggest improving the relational makeup of the policy environment.

Mark Smith laments the pervasive logic of standardisation, introduced for reasons of management control in public services, because it is incapable of absorbing variety, while prohibiting service work to walk the 'extra mile', which he maintains has become the new norm. By the end of his essay there is some recognition that 'some' services benefit from 'some' standardisation, but the danger of standardisation is its associated focus on method and procedures, rather than substantive problem-solving as a relational exercise, not a hierarchical one. Similarly, Catherine Needham challenges the orthodoxy of professionalisation into siloed care services, helping professionals to stay out of court, in an era where citizenship diversity requires integrated solutions of work, care, health and housing support, again in a relational fashion. As Smith does in the previous chapter, in her conclusion Needham warns us not to junk professional expertise altogether, in an advocacy for self-managed care teams of about 10 professionals supporting 50 neighbourhood patients to address wicked care problems in an integrated fashion.

Jake Hayman abhors the universal disconnect in the world of philanthropy, where 'city' involvement, based on a trickle-down paradigm of spreadsheet monitoring, is driving out joined-up activities designed to bolster communities, whilst ignoring deep problems of inequality. Stephen Lock's heresy also points in the direction of the failure of 'organisation' in solving community problems, because organisations create hierarchical control by managers, directors and policy makers. What the world needs now, he argues, is less control and more genuine networking for better results. He also admits that effective networks often comprise many organisations, as in the NHS, but what matters is how interconnected organisations coalesce around a shared purpose on the basis of reciprocity and trust, which is the lifeblood that makes effective networks adaptive and resilient.

Most heretical perhaps is the proposal, based on the finance lessons of the Great Recession, by Vincent Richardson and Alan Peyton, to give government the monopoly on money creation. Lax financial regulation created a global money bubble that was destined to burst. When it did, the state had to rescue the 'too big to fail' banks but, once salvaged, banks were reluctant to increase lending because of the lack of economic demand. Once more, the doom-loop had to be resolved through state intervention in the form of quantitative easing or simply money creation. Subsequent trials and tribulations surely beg the question: "why we do not make money creation the unique competence of the state, in order to ease recessions and forestall bank runs?"

In their respective heresies, both Peter Wright and Richard Davis take on the issue of the evidential bases for policy. Richard Davis reiterates some of the insights from Smith, Needham and Lock – that managers always measure the wrong things, mainly those relating to control, budgets and accountability rather than those relating to the more fundamental questions of problem-solving in helping people to lead flourishing lives. Peter Wright boldly states that evidence is never good enough in the sense that for evidence to capture the hearts and minds of citizens and policy makers, it has to be anchored in a persuasive political narrative with a strong sense of purpose. Only then will the evidence become actionable in terms of reform, given the limited attention span of policy makers and the ever-present danger of regulatory capture.

Striking in all the heresies in this volume is how the relevant institutional status quo is unequivocally described as perverted. This immediately raises the question of whether – if we are able to persuade policy makers to change their plans as we wish – this will actually bring about massive improvements as things inescapably continue to change. How can we be sure that a state monopoly of money creation will lead to optimal investments in the real economy? Do open networks work better than rigidified organisation on all counts? Can we really do away with state capacity beyond money creation? This brings me back to the rise and fall of Keynesian economics in the 20th century. In the 1920s, John Maynard Keynes fought Marshallian mainstream classical economics as a true heretic. He received widespread recognition after the Great Depression for having vindicated macroeconomics: the study of the behaviour of the economy as a whole (rather than the sum of the microeconomic behaviour of individuals, households and firms) as a branch of economics in its own right. As a heretic, Keynes portrayed counter-cyclical management as a 'general' theory to replace existing policy beliefs. However, with the benefit of hindsight, I would say that Keynesian macroeconomics added up to no more than a very important 'sometimes true' theory, relevant to the historical exigencies of the Great Depression and, more recently, the Great Recession. Keynesianism was discarded in the 1980s against the background of runaway inflation and rising unemployment, which monetarism and rational-expectation macroeconomics proved better able to explain. Equally revealing is that the fallout from the financial crisis also relegated monetarism to 'sometimes true' status. My take is that we live in a world of only 'sometimes true' theories, but in order to receive policy-making attention, we have sell our ideas as 'general' ones.

If we *do* live in world of merely 'sometimes-true' theories, this should have practical relevance. There is no denying the importance to actors of the structural incentives and constraints presented by the institutional environment in which they live. And while environmental changes alter the functioning of existing institutions, based on current 'sometimes true' theories, they also modify the interests and preferences of relevant political actors and their relative power positions to (re-)enforce their objectives in various directions. Let's face it, the economic, social and political worlds are messy, and dynamic interactions create equilibria as much as diversity and turbulence. This harbours consequences for academics. We should be humble, in the first place; we should respect the non-linear dynamic complexity of the social world we study, expand our time horizons, pay attention to what is institutionally relevant, with a strong focus on linking substantive problem-solving, and accept that governance structures will follow suit only sluggishly. The suitability of any governance framework ultimately depends on the substantive task at hand. Since substantive exigencies change over time, there is no single best governance solution in the offing. Therefore, we should be modest and acknowledge that we (can) master 'sometimes true' theories institutionally 'somehow'. This sobering conclusion leads me to advocate creating permanent learning by building monitoring devices into our democratic polities to somehow help us to try to learn ahead of failure.

Editorial

At the beginning of the introduction to our previous edited collection, we said this was an unconventional book for unconventional times. In retrospect it seems we were both right and wrong about that. Correct in the sense that many of the signs in 2016 indicated the end of an era, as the apparent final thrashings of new public management (NPM) and the cult of measurement was consistently skewered by our heretics from a range of positions in policy and practice. One of them described the concept of measuring 'wellbeing' as 'neoliberalism in a fluffy pink dress'. However, we were also incorrect about the extent to which the changes we have seen since then have perhaps raised the stakes even higher in terms of what the future direction might be.

As a result of what has happened over the last four years, we feel even more committed to the importance of heresy in public policy than we were before. Partially it was due to the positive responses we have had to the concept. Reviews of the book welcomed the 'powerful thread' of the critique of those making policy mimicking private sector practices (Tizard 2016) and the ways in which our authors work made visible our shared 'complex social reality' and the ways in which our current approaches lead to 'chronically suboptimal outcomes' (St Denny, 2018). We were also buoyed by interest in the heresy approach from colleagues across the world including New Zealand (Wellington) and the Republic of Ireland (Trinity College). We were challenged to be even more challenging!

At the point of writing this introduction it remains unclear what the policy direction is likely to be for public services. Given the initial rhetoric of the new UK government, the likelihood of significant movement in the directions set out by our first tranche of heretics seems unlikely, in England at least. However, hope springs eternal as, it seems, at the heart of government lie people with a strong agenda for change of what they regard as the failed structure and mechanics of the state and the need for improved accountability to the people. Subsequent events, in the form of the global lockdown at the hands of leaders of all shades, have demonstrated that the unthinkable has become the incredibly do-able in the face of a pandemic. Whatever this turns out to mean in reality, there are points of light on the horizon:

- Our heretics continue to respond to the challenge of participating in a wider movement, making work and society fairer and more equitable though change.
- The campaigning of Children England led by Kathy Evans highlighting the imminent collapse of care services in local government and the need to address the failed marketisation of children's services.
- The work of Toby Lowe, who has established a movement called the 'Human Learning System' approach to bring together those seeking to cultivate the alternative to the 'system' of centralised control and measure approach, which is so prevalent in our public services that it is an invisible force (Lowe et al, 2017, 2019).
- The continuing challenge to orthodoxy from Sue White and Dave Wastell on the application of 'science' as evidence for the justification for early intervention.
- Simon Guilfoyle's critiquing of targets in policing (Guilfoyle, 2013).
- Simon Duffy's work at the Centre for Welfare Reform on Universal Credit (www.centreforwelfarereform.org).
- John Seddon and his colleagues at Vanguard continue the war against command and control management. John's latest book, *Beyond Command and Control*, represents everything John has learned to date having worked on the ground since the 1980s in a range of dysfunctional service organisations.
- Simon Caulkin continues to blog about the problems caused by monolithic approaches to change and management at simoncaulkin.com
- Stephen Crossley remains a fierce critic of the 'Troubled Families' programme and his recent book was published by Policy Press (Crossley, 2018).

Our heretics in this volume echo many themes from the first, including the critiques of performance management that Cathy Hobbs deliciously describes as a long-term 'distraction' for those working in public services who lost the focus on the bigger picture. She prescribes slowing down and focussing on learning for improvement. Richard Davis continues on this thread using examples from his career in consultancy of how managers consistently measure the wrong things. Challenges to the current system structures come from Catherine Needham and Steve Lock who call out professionals and organisations as barriers for change. Next, the thought-provoking chapter from Richardson and Peyton who suggest that the government needs to take direct control of the money in the economy. Another heretic in this vein is Jake Hayman who explains how charitable giving is broken as a result of the connection between mission and service delivery being lost in the race to evidence impact. Also, on this theme, the chapter from Peter Wright who uses the recent history of government public health policies around alcohol to claim that evidence isn't enough to make policy due to the dark interests in stopping us doing the right thing. Finally, we have the chapter from Mark Smith whose dual heresy is the apparent paradox that standardisation of services is more costly than personalisation and that bespoke provision (not 'one-stop shops') is the way ahead if we are to reduce failure demand.

The aim of the heresy series remains to offer a public platform for challenging the assumptions of current orthodoxies. The heretics we have selected for the book all make contributions to the idea that there is an alternative way of organising and thinking about public policy challenges. In one of the most centralised states in Europe we await the required shift from the government paradigm which emphasises competition over co-operation, marketisation over communities, the national over local, individuality over relationships, and performance management over learning.

The current crisis has been demonstrably exacerbated by these trite transactional approaches to society, in which efficiency rules. We see the potential of a positive, relationship-based approach in the everyday courage that is visible at the time of writing at the height of the Covid-19 pandemic in the action of key workers of the state, in business and voluntary organisations and in the community at large. Some parts of the political and media machine describe our situation as a state of war. This may or may not be misguided but, make no mistake, history shows that those who survive such wars demand an improvement in conditions for themselves, their families, their communities and society as a whole when normal life resumes. The point here is that it cannot be the old normal. Our heretics and their words remain prescient and we look forward to a time (which has perhaps just drawn nearer) when such ideas are no longer heresies but the basis of new orthodoxies which, as the author of our Foreword, Anton Hemerijck, sagely tells us, can and should only ever be 'sometime true'.

Rob Wilson, Charlotte Pell, Toby Lowe and Jan Myers
April 2020

References:

Crossley, S. (2018) *Troublemakers: The Construction of 'Troubled Families' as a Social Problem*, Policy Press

Evans, Kathy: https://www.childrenengland.org.uk

Guilfoyle, S. (2013) *Intelligent Policing*, Triarchy Press

Lowe, T. & Plimmer, D. (2017) *A Whole New World — Funding and Commissioning in Complexity*, Collaborate

Lowe,T. & Plimmer. D. (2019) 'Exploring the new world: practical insights for funding, commissioning and managing in complexity', Collaborate

Seddon, J. et al. (2019) *Beyond Command and Control*, Vanguard Consulting Ltd.

St. Denny, E. (2018) 'Kittens are evil: Little heresies in public policy', *Local Government Studies*, 44:3, 438-441, DOI: 10.1080/03003930.2018.1475169

Tizard, J. (2016) 'Review of Kittens are Evil', *Municipal Journal*

Wastell, D. and White, S. (2017) *Blinded by Science: The Social Implications of Epigenetics and Neuroscience*, Policy Press

The editors would like to acknowledge the support of the Centre for Knowledge Innovation Technology and Enterprise (KITE) at Newcastle University and the support at our new home Newcastle Business School at Northumbria University.

Bespoke by Default: The Future for Public Services

Mark Smith

Director of Public Service Reform, Gateshead Council

Services to the public are in need of reform. This is not simply because there is a shortage of money. It is not due to a lack of skills. It is not a lack of ability or motivation. Nor is it due to an increase in demand, because there is already a collective capacity to deal with much more than we are dealing with and to do so more effectively.

It is because there is a pervasive root logic in the way we see work and how we organise and operate things – a root logic that is at odds with working in a way that simply gets things right for people.

The logic has become so pervasive that citizens now expect that things won't be handled at the point of interaction, that decisions will take days or weeks (when they could actually take minutes), that they will only get help when things are 'bad enough' or that they will have to make appointments for things rather than access help when they need and are able to.

Society *gets* that 'computer says no' because *systems* say no so very often. Public sector workers have become accustomed to defaulting to 'no' and resorting to 'yes'. So it has reached a point where many citizens will actually temper their demands: second-guessing what things can be reasonably asked for.

Why would a recently widowed tenant ask to move from one social housing property to another when all she really needs is some help with the garden? Why couldn't she just ask for that? What logic is at play here? How did it come to this?

Moreover, there is astonishment and there are plaudits when good people, stuck working in a less-than-good system, go 'off-script' to help people in ways that are reasonable and thoughtful. We often call it the 'extra mile' and have essentially institutionalised such an attitude as exceptional.

But why is the 'extra mile' extra at all? It should be normal. It should be how we do what we do. After all, this is what people are generally like and they want to be like this at work.

What kind of logic causes us to suspend what we know and who we are, to accept something less as how things have to be?

This logic is a devotion to standards

Standards have to stop blighting our thinking whenever we talk about services. Standards are not compatible with service. Sadly though, but not irreversibly, this is seen as heresy by many in public services and public policy.

It's in our everyday lexicon... "We have standards you know" ... and we take from this received wisdom that it assures us of goodness. 'Standards' have become conflated with 'quality', but they are not the same.

A default, standardised amount of something or a fixed and repeatable approach to a problem that innately varies (and if anything varies, it's people) removes an opportunity to apply judgement and nuance, drawing on experience and an appraisal of what matters to whomever needs help. Standards fixate around one key judgement: does it meet the standard?

The priority given to standards over time dulls judgement, deskills, clouds perspective, demotivates and, most worryingly of all, distracts from our ability to empathise and even to want to empathise.

Standards destroy morale and obliterate creativity, which is especially hampering when people's context, their *stories*, vary so very much.

But there is much cause for hope. People are adept at dealing with subtle yet important variations in what matters. It is this talent for absorbing variety, rather than looking for what is defendable, that should form the base logic behind services to people who need them to help live better lives.

If we make our ability to understand people and to solve problems the DNA of the design of public services then we can be *bespoke by default* – surely the utopia for public services and for our society as a whole.

The orthodoxy: standards as a means to efficiency

Standardisation as a logic appears in three broad ways in service systems:

1 – What you get: a standard or fixed offer

2 – How you get it: a standard operating procedure or fixed method

3 – Who gets it: a standard filter or fixed eligibility criteria

These aren't mutually exclusive; indeed, most service systems have examples of more than one of them.

The orthodoxy goes that these three approaches to deploying standards provide managers with a means of control and can create efficiencies. They can also result in delusions of fairness, where equality (giving everyone the same thing) and equity (acting proportionately to reflect varying needs) are confused.

These three tools induce some signature management behaviours, such as very diligent process design (e.g. flow charts and decision trees), a clear and documented view of compliance (e.g. scripts) and performance management mechanisms that test workers for compliance (e.g. mystery shopping and activity-based performance indicators).

It is an ***energetic pursuit of laziness***. The energy is deployed in the boardroom or the project room, somewhere a citizen isn't. The detail and plausibility induce feelings of confidence and produce materials that pertain to quality. It looks good! Customers will just flow through it, right?

It's also very trainable. The standard playbook for the system is written, so the job of management is now seemingly to ensure the right standard plays are deployed to the right customers. These plays are likely to be a combination of fixed offers, methods and eligibility. It being trainable also makes it very inspectable – so employees know how they should respond if they are to survive.

So when creating standards, huge amounts of energy are deployed before the customer actually presents. This energetic pursuit gives way to laziness once the customer gets involved. Here, it's just a matter of inspecting for compliance and rewarding and punishing employees accordingly. This is the efficiency that is strived for – turn the handle and off it goes.

It is management by algorithm; a series of 'if-then-else's' not too dissimilar to computer code. Clues to seek out are 'pathways', 'protocols' or 'standard operating procedures'.

When there are enough of these in one place, they become the core ingredients of 'target operating models' (TOMs) – plausible and transferable blueprints that give hope to beleaguered leaders and income to canny consultancies. Such operating models essentially see large organisations dealing with complex problems rather like large train-sets, i.e. they take a bit of setting up, but run smoothly once the switch is flicked.

If only it were so simple.

This could only be even plausible if everybody went through life on predictable, shapeable tracks whilst being ever reliable and consistent. They don't and they aren't, but standards dupe us into thinking that they could be, and we design for this. If the target is being ineffective and defensive, you'll hit the jackpot with a TOM.

Where did the heresy come from? Why do we standardise services?

Before service became an industry, the only large-scale industry was manufacturing. Standards have a glorious past and a central role to play in manufacturing. Manufacturing things that make our lives easier and fun in vast quantities at very low unit costs depends upon standardisation.

The process of making something time and again efficiently and with few errors does not usually involve the customer and so their innate variation does not become a factor to design into a manufacturing system.

The people who pioneered manufacturing are still household names and they were the first captains of industry. They did remarkable things and it is no surprise that they got to write the textbook on organisational development, process design and quality. After all, they changed the world.

But when service followed as a large-scale industry in its own right, the perhaps not-unreasonable-at-the-time thing to do was to use the manufacturing playbook and to bring standards into service design. As our desire and need for service becomes ever more nuanced and as there are more and more of us, the playbook soon gets strained, but the pioneering nature of it means its logic plays into a commonly held world view to this day.

Manufacturing has cast a huge standardisation shadow over service for the simple reason that it came first. Which is why the view of standards that I am proposing here is a heresy in the first place.

Who holds with the orthodoxy?

Standardisation is the Japanese Knotweed of logics. It is hard to dislodge, spreads quickly and is everywhere.

Standards are easy to describe and inspect and, as a result, people readily hold them dear. MBAs, professional accreditations and regulatory inspections are all built upon a bedrock of standardisation. How public service organisations are judged by formal inspectorates very much matters to them and so, for better or for worse, most public service organisations end up institutionalising standards.

Standards make it easy to compare our numbers with those of other organisations. This gains traction in a regulatory and inspection-rich environment because such comparisons help to create and maintain defendable positions. This quickly becomes the game, and the hope of absorbing citizen variety rapidly fades. It is easy to criticise leaders in this space but it is only human to want to survive when the inspectors come calling, armed with standards and with genuine power.

It is no wonder that this is a firmly held belief or accepted way to work when so much rides upon doing it well.

Worryingly, it has become normalised in us as citizens, whether or not we care about the nuances of service design and performance. Our near constant exposure to standards and their consequences has shaped our thinking and expectations rather insidiously.

This has the curious effect of making simple things appear complicated or in some way inspired. Doing the right thing and opting out of an obviously sub-optimal, pre-determined standard becomes the extra mile rather than a clue as to how to make doing the right thing much more possible and indeed, quite normal.

I was once party to a request from a woman who called her local council because she wanted to have some bulky waste collected. As things stood, she would have needed to wait 10 days or so for her neighbourhood to be on the bulky waste collection rota and the script began to kick in around what she would have to do and not do in the meantime. She interjected, quickly adding that, sadly, her husband was due to leave hospital imminently and he was coming home to die. This meant creating space for a hospital bed and other equipment as soon as was possible. The call centre operative put the lady on hold and called the bulky waste collection team and between them, they arranged for the pick-up to be done within a few hours.

Rightly, this was lauded. It was off system, done bespoke and was based on a human understanding of what matters. It was the extra mile in action.

Standard offers, procedures and eligibility were designed into the substantive system (we're coming on this date, we'll only collect these things and only if we find them perfectly dry, outside the house, bagged and sealed just so, etc...). Responding to demands according to what suited customers was clearly non-standard operating procedure.

The seemingly heretical moral of this tale is almost too simple to be credible to those mired in standards: if we study demand from everyone and understand what matters to them, we stand a chance of designing a system that is as close to perfect as possible for everyone. If we continue to adhere to a fixed standard, we stand zero chance and we only do the right thing by exception and blind luck.

Bulky waste collection is competitive and income generating, so there is a further opportunity to find out what matters to those that are not customers but could be (those that use competitors, perhaps even those who 'resort' to fly tipping so that designing them in as customers solves two problems...). To paraphrase W. Edwards Deming, would understanding what a bespoke system might look like be an opportunity to allow your customers to pull you away from the competition?

What is the heresy?

Let's postulate that organisations do things on a continuum, with *making things* at one end through to *carrying out simple transactions* for people somewhere in the middle and *helping them to solve their problems* at the other end.

The orthodoxy is that standardisation has a role to play right across this continuum. The heresy is that it does not. Instead, problem solving requires that we become bespoke by default when we seek to help solve problems through the medium of services and relationships. Standardisation helps when making and fixing, not solving and helping.

However, it is not a total heresy. It's not quite as simple as saying that standards work for making and bespoke is the only way for doing. The cusps between bespoke and standardisation and between service and manufacturing are offset.

This is because there are some services that *do* benefit from a degree of standardisation, but it is important to understand that they are of a type. They are simple processes and require no expertise to administer. They have a small number of variables and are essentially repeatable transactions that provide a degree of service.

Examples include taxing a vehicle, booking a squash court and changing currencies. They require no manufacturing but would show efficiencies through applying some standards.

These processes (essentially transactions) are high-volume and this does present something of a trap. This 'transaction trap' is to take any successes derived from applying standardisation to simple, high-volume transactions as a reason to apply the orthodoxy to all service types as a matter of course and to seek to standardise services that have more causes of variation and thus require a bespoke approach.

Could it be that we should standardise social care assessments? No. Not if the intention is to understand every person that we are trying to help. Alas, the current rigidity around eligibility criteria is an example of where standardisation reaches for a target and misses the point.

Standardisation and digital

A good example of the 'transaction trap' is how some in local government have interpreted the opportunities presented by the emerging digital agenda. Much of the excitement and energy around digitising services in the public sector has come from digitising those transactions that fall within this 'overlap'. To some, the hope was that automation would cover a huge amount of traffic, saving money on employees and saving time for citizens. This is because digitisation and standardisation are comfortable bedfellows: coding software to encompass already codified processes.

The orthodoxy suggests standardisation has a role everywhere, and thus, by extension, digital solutions are seen as having the potential to hardwire a large number of standard processes right through to the end-user via self-service. If this were the case, we could apply even more energy to the pursuit of even more laziness, with machines dealing with just about every interaction as if it were a transaction. This would mean service organisations committing a lot of money and energy to setting up the latest, most technologically advanced train-set to deploy their services.

But to do this would be to misunderstand what technology and digital bring to the table and to misapply standards to services. Technology's key offer boils down to its ability to move information around more quickly to more people in more places. It cannot absorb variety anything like as well as a human because we're as quirky and variable as it gets.

A useful way of describing the relationship between standardisation and digital is to consider who ought to be the user of technology for any given demand. The demands that are simple and require no expertise are those for which the *citizen* could use technology to interact with an organisation. The demands that are more complex with more variables to consider might be helped by technology if the *employee* uses it to do their job in the course of helping the citizen (e.g. accessing information that they judge to be useful, recording information that enables ongoing help and for others to pitch in, etc.). This means doing bespoke quickly and accurately via human interaction and backed up with good and accessible information.

The orthodoxy of standardisation across the whole continuum of service and manufacturing can lead to the creation of digital programmes, which seek to *maximise* the deployment of technology to citizens. Instead, applying the heresy of 'bespoke by default' translates this into *optimising* the deployment of technology either to citizens or to those employees whose purpose is to help them.

Why this heresy matters and is a road to reform

When standardisation is applied to problems requiring a bespoke approach to both understand and solve, it fails to work. Not only does this mean that citizens continue to have problems, it also creates more demand because it is highly likely that they will re-present and with more urgency.

This is an *amplification* of demand generated by the design of public services. It is both the greatest cause of strain and the best opportunity for reform.

Working with people *bespoke* to help solve their problems so that they do not re-present so often is the most sustainable route to reform. What's compelling about this is that it is something people can do. After all, people already knew how to arrange for a same day collection of bulky waste for a family who needed it out of the way right now.

No amount of sharing of services and fine-tuning of processes and management restructures will act on the cause of some of society's most pressing and difficult problems. It is acting on the cause of problems that will lead to reduction in demand and create adaptive, purposeful services for those that need them. More importantly, it requires the development of strong and relevant relationships between citizen, communities and state.

Changing how we change

Efforts to reform typically start with changes to governance and structures; meetings to agree scope, to marshal project resources and to create timelines. To adopt this heresy, the starting point has instead to focus initially upon *method*, specifically: how can we systematically help people with long-standing and/or complex and/or multiple problems?

Only once we have learned how to be effective (solve problems, reduce/prevent re-presentation) can we hope to learn how to be efficient. Efficiency begins when methods that work form into roles, principles and measures. It is only beyond this point that we can hope to make it sustainable.

Governance and structures are what allow systems and services to be sustained, but it must first be understood what it is that needs sustaining.

This means that making the change to bespoke by default requires a reversal in the usual order of change programmes, with governance and structures coming last, not first.

Making the change to bespoke by default

There is much to learn. If we know innately how to understand and help people, then an ecosystem of services to the public that knows how to understand people and draw upon the skills and capacity to help them should not be something too lofty to aim for.

To do this, we need to liberate skills, knowledge and authority to be where they need to be to help people.

This is difficult to do when the focus is forcibly upon standards. For example, standards lead to assessing rather than understanding. An assessment generally asks, 'How much of what we do, can we do to you?' This is a very different question from one that which solves problems, which is, 'What does a good life for you look like?' This distinction describes well the differences between deploying standards and solving problems through a bespoke approach.

The road to reform through bespoke approaches means not the abandonment of standards, but their restriction to one-dimensional, repeatable transactions. Instead, skills, knowledge and authority should be present at the point at which work is done.

Recently, I was fortunate to witness an officer in a council 'go rogue' by responding differently to a non-payment of Council Tax. Instead of the official letter and threat of court, plus the layering on of more costs due to court proceedings, bailiffs, etc. (purpose = get our money), he contacted the woman in question. He did this because he could see that there had been attempts to pay but they were inconsistent. He was immediately off standard process.

He learned of a single mum with three kids, all of whom were struggling at school; he learned she was working long hours and had to rely on the children's grandmother for childcare, which was creating new strains. He learned that there were also some rent arrears and there was also a toxic relationship with a neighbour, which meant home life was always difficult and it was a large part of why the children were unsettled.

He learned that the answer was to move, but the standard operating procedure was that you could not move from one social housing property to another with rent arrears. Housing and Council Tax employees took a bespoke approach in moving them anyway whilst agreeing a workable plan to pay off the debts. She continues to work and is also training to improve her prospects. The debts are steadily being settled and she and her family have a chance.

The standard process would have seen them in court, with more debts and having a miserable time. Bespoke was cheaper, recovered more of the debt (and will continue to) and means that the three children have more of a chance to succeed and to be happy. The demands from her and her children that were prevented are considerable. It also had a huge impact on the morale of those involved.

This work has grown into a prototype which explored abandoning standards, referrals, assessments and any received wisdom for which there was no evidence and started with the problem to be solved from the point of view of the citizen. We learned that relationships solve problems, not hierarchies. We learned that creating the freedom for empathy and relationship-building systematically led to innovation (not sometimes, but always) and we learned that the sky did not fall in when we abandoned standards.

This is compassion, intrinsic motivation and judgement. It's not code-able, exactly predictable or easily trainable but it is something that the vast majority of people already know how to do. It is the difference between assessing someone and understanding them. This is the root to effectiveness and the place to start reforming services to the public.

~

Mark Smith is Director of Public Service Reform at Gateshead Council

Death of the Professional: The Future is Generic

Catherine Needham

Professor of Public Policy and Public Management, University of Birmingham

"Professionalism will be the death of local government. It's that lack of ability to soften and shape stuff according to locality."
(Local government interviewee cited in Needham & Mangan, 2014)

What is the orthodoxy that you are challenging?

Within my sights here are the professionals who deliver our public services. That includes some of the traditional professions: medicine, law, accountancy, teaching. But it also includes more modern professions like social work and nursing. I would also like to include housing officers and librarians, police officers and the fire service. These are, to varying degrees, knowledge workers, whose roles include aspects of the professions: a body of knowledge and expertise, codes of ethics, altruism, rationality (Exworthy, 1998). They vary in the extent to which they require that other aspect of the traditional professions, high quality educational credentials, and they are not all regulated as the professions traditionally are. But they contain within them a discourse of what it means to do a job *professionally,* which I argue is about deploying a particular domain of expertise and set of behaviours (Evans, 2016).

Where and by whom is it held

The traditional professions, exemplified by bowler-hatted men crossing London Bridge to work as lawyers, doctors and medics, feel like an antiquated bunch. But the boundaries around professional roles remain alive and well within different domains of public sector work. Royal Colleges, professional bodies such as the General Medical Council, unions such as the British Medical Association and sector bodies like Skills for Care and Skills for Health uphold certain entry requirements and skill sets so that the public can be reassured when they are dealing with a doctor, a social worker or a lawyer that the people have the appropriate training. Suggestions that ancillary roles might be able to take on some of the work of professionals are always met with howls of opposition.

There has been some recognition of the ways in which professional roles have changed. For example, because of the impact of technology, as Susskind and Susskind (2015) argue, the notion of traditional professions, clearly demarcated from each other, is eroding. Michael Saks (2013) argues that we have gone from the metaphor of a zoo – in which clearly distinguished professional groupings were kept apart by legal monopolies with registers creating insiders and excluding outsiders – to a safari park, where professionals roam around interacting and overlapping with each other. We are left with a fuzzy concept – Kevin Morrell (2007) calls it a 'folk concept' of the professions – which focuses on people who occupy a particular status based on privileged access to a body of knowledge. It is the broad group of public service workers who have a claim on being professional that is my focus here.

What is your heresy?

We are witnessing the death of the professions as a distinct and separate category of workers, and this should be celebrated: the future is generic. The very notion of separate professionals is antithetical to the sorts of 'whole person' support that public services need to deliver (Hudson, 2015). The education and regulation of professionals as separate cadres of workers leads to an approach in treating individuals using public services as a distinct set of service specifications: a health need or a housing need or a care need. We know that sustained improvements in people's lives require holistic responses, and that so-called wicked problems cannot be solved through segmented solutions (Rittel & Webber, 1973). And we know that the relationships that people have at the frontlines of public service are best when they are sustained and enable continuity and breadth (Bickerstaffe, 2013; Clancy & Duffy, 2013; Frank, 2013; WHO, 2015). Changing citizen expectations of public services has encouraged some boundary spanning, as 'tell us once' and 'one stop shop' initiatives have sought to make services more integrated and customer friendly (Asgarkhani, 2005). These changes require different ways of working with citizens. But often these are triage services, designed to assess whether and which of the specialist professionals working behind the scenes should be asked to support the person.

I argue that we are moving to a point where what is needed in public services is not so much a set of specialists, each holding on to their distinct sets of knowledge and practices, but a generalist, equipped to engage with citizens in different kinds of ways. Public services will thrive or wither depending on the extent to which they recognise this change.

We can see the fire service as the canary in the mine, telling us how public service work with citizens is changing. When my friend John joined the fire service twenty years ago he joined a service where most of the role was emergency work – fires obviously, but other crisis situations like road traffic accidents, along with the occasional cat up a tree and a stall at the local school summer fair.

This became a problem when things didn't catch fire any more. The invention of oven chips, the decline in smoking and the growth in flame retardant furniture reduced the prevalence of house fires. Car security increased and teenagers were too busy on their Play Stations to go out and set cars on fire anyway. With occasional tragic exceptions, fires became a much less significant aspect of the work of the fire service.

The Marmot Review of Health Inequalities in 2010 highlighted the important role that the fire service could play in more preventative work within communities. A good example of this is the 'sloppy slippers' campaign run by the fire service, which targeted falls prevention in older people's homes. These kinds of preventative services have since grown in scope. Every week firefighters will go into people's homes, looking at smoke alarms and trip hazards, although this work is not limited to traditional safety checks. Many fire services now hold contracts from the local authority for public health work in which, as well as telling them not to smoke in bed, they also ask people about debt management, diet and mental health (NHS England, 2015).

The expertise and behaviours that my friend John needs to be good at this kind of role are potentially very different from those of traditional emergency-oriented fire service work. Whereas in an emergency situation you are the person with the power – a command and control approach – when someone is letting you into their home, the power is much more equally shared. When you are asking people about sensitive topics – are they lonely? do they drink too much? – you need a set of 'soft skills', communication skills, rapport building. It is a form of emotional labour – to use the concept developed by Hothschild (1983) – but one which is very different to the emotional toll of emergency response, and which we don't yet know enough about how to value and support.

Why are you right, and why is the orthodoxy wrong?

The rising awareness of the 'emotion work' of public service and of the ways in which effective public service requires boundary spanning, highlights the significance of a generic skill set which is different from the technical skill set which has been valued in public services in the past (Needham et al., 2017). Skills of communication, organisation and caring become more highly prized. Davidson writes about 'twenty-first century literacies'. These include: interpersonal skills (facilitation, empathy, political skills); synthesising skills (sorting evidence, analysis, making judgements, offering critique and being creative); organising skills for group work, collaboration and peer review; communication skills, making better use of new media and multi-media resources (Davidson, 2011). This more relational way of working has been the focus of recent reports from the IPPR, Participle and others (Cookle & Muir, 2012; Muir & Parker, 2014; Cottam, 2011). However, the workforce elements of a relational approach to public services have not been explored in depth. As one interviewee put it, for research that Catherine Mangan and I undertook for *The 21st Century Public Servant*, "Dealing with people in a more relational way is a skill that will need to be developed." (Needham & Mangan, 2014).

Why am I talking about the fire service? Because the skills that you now need to succeed in the fire service have changed substantially – in ways that are also affecting other people working in public services. To illustrate the ways in which I see public service work as changing, *The 21st Century Public Servant* focused on the roles and skills needed for the public service workforce. By interviewing people working in a cross section of public service organisations (including in the private and third sectors), we identified a number of factors at work which were shaping the way that people saw their work.

As one interviewee put it, "We need more skills as the council becomes smaller – not just professional skills but facilitators, good questioners, coaches." There may be a need for more generic analytical skills than has been realised in the past: "Some of the things around engaging with citizens and the use, analysis and interpretation of data to understand your local populations, they are quite newish sets of skills for people who work in local authorities." Another saw the future this way: "In the future we won't have structures that are wholly lawyers, HR professionals. People will have to be able to manage across different professional groups."

What has to change, and who has to change it?

We need public services that support the relational, and that may require rethinking the scale of public service organisations. Big organisations in the public and private sectors as a rule prioritise the efficient processing of people – the customer service algorithm – rather than the building and sustaining of relationships. In some settings that's OK: we know that large specialist hospitals can be safer than smaller ones because the high volume of interventions means staff are very experienced and there is a critical mass of expertise in one place. But lots of public services are formed at the point of interaction between the person and the provider of the service, the teacher, the nurse, the care worker. And creating and sustaining good relationships on a small scale needs to be a priority. Laloux's work (2014) on reinventing organisations suggests that the future of organisations is to support self-organisation and self-management. Assigned positions and job descriptions are replaced by a multiplicity of fluid roles. Organisations are highly adaptive, adjusting to better meet the organisations' purpose.

The way we recruit people also needs to change. In our 21st Century Public Servant work, several interviewees suggested that current HR practices are too rigid to enable a flexible and agile workforce, or to provide organisations with the skills they need when they need them. Interviewees commented that traditionally HR professionals tended to focus on the narrow procedural issues of recruitment rather the wider workforce planning: "it's all about how do we keep ourselves out of the courts, not about planning our future workforce". Others suggested that we need to translate the strategic picture into something that HR professionals doing the recruitment can understand:

> In recruitment we ask for the easy things, experience of delivering a housing repair service, knowledge-based things. And maybe it is more about asking about innovation – how have they changed a culture, impacted on a policy, introduced a new idea.

Recruiting to different criteria was seen as important. One interviewee said:

It's about recognising and rewarding the wider competencies which aren't about the kind of job you do but the kind of person you are.'

According to another:

We have always done values-based recruitment, tested out values in recruitment, but that really just meant a question in an interview that people learned the right answer to. We are now working with Skills for Care on recruitment and retention tools around values.

Thinking differently about the size and structure of public service organisations does then create an opportunity to recruit, train and develop different kinds of public servants. An example comes from Local Area Coordination (lacnetwork.org), an approach to early intervention which has been introduced in several local authorities after being successfully developed in Australia. The LAC model seeks to deliver a proactive and person-centred approach to support which combines elements of community development with care management. The coordinator is expected to give wide-ranging assistance rather than splitting care, health, housing and other issues into separate service streams (Glasby, 2014; Kahana et al., 2011; Laragy et al., 2015). Recruitment to such a role emphasises the cross-cutting nature of the job where "Coordinators also provided information, assisted people in building their support networks, and helped people to purchase their own supports via direct consumer funding" (Lord & Hutchison, 2003).

Of course, the growth of this more generic workforce cannot mean junking professional expertise altogether. We still need the expert emergency skills of fire fighters, and the precision skills of surgeons. The insights of social workers about family dynamics, or of librarians about the curation of information, cannot be wholly replaced by an army of generic workers whose excellent soft skills can make up for a lack of deep knowledge. The challenge then is how to layer these skills, so that we retain people with expertise, but acknowledge that much of their job will not be about deploying that specialist knowledge. If we take early intervention and preventative, whole-person approaches seriously, then we will minimise (though not remove) the need for more downstream skills.

An example of effective layering comes from the Buurtzorg nursing model in the Netherlands (and which is being adapted and introduced in parts of the UK as Wellbeing Teams (http://bit.ly/kittens06). Buurtzorg has

8,000 trained nurses providing care across the country to people who need ongoing support at home due to frailty and ill-health (Gray et al., 2015). Buurtzorg nurses work in self-managed teams of 10-12 people, with no management outside the team (although coaches are available). Each team supports around 50 patients within a neighbourhood. What is distinctive about the Buurtzorg model is that it emphasises a holistic type of care in which highly trained nurses help with everything that is needed by a frail older person or a person with a long-term health condition or disability. Thus nurses will dress bandages and dispense medicines, but they will also hang out washing, prepare food and link people up with their neighbours. In doing so, the workers are not adhering to the professional norms of nursing which emphasise a clinical role, and clear differential from ancillary care staff.

Public service employers need to create more opportunities to develop initiatives like Local Area Coordination and Buurtzorg-type initiatives. People trying to get these off the ground in localities note that they have to make the case again and again for approaches which have been evaluated thoroughly elsewhere (Fox, 2017). We need to get better at being willing to get on with these approaches and let the evidence base catch up. Good enough approaches to evidencing interventions are already out there and need to be used more flexibly (Durose et al., 2017).

Conclusion

I have offered here an account of why we should think differently about public service careers and skills sets if we are to deliver on the promise of whole-person approaches and make progress on addressing the so-called wicked problems that underpin them. Of course it's important not to be naïve about the knowledge base needed by public servants, but we need to rethink public services for a context in which the deep, specialist knowledge is complemented by broad skills which cross service boundaries and develop strong supportive relationships with individuals and communities.

This will mean recruiting, training and rewarding people in different ways, and has implications for how we educate and prepare entrants into the workforce for the careers that await them. If fire service recruitment leaflets still show people in full emergency gear up high ladders putting out fires then entrants to the role risk being poorly prepared for the day-to-day work that awaits them.

It will also mean thinking differently about the organisations in which we locate public service work. Large bureaucracies thrive on role demarcations and mechanistic metaphors. They struggle to value and reward people who work across boundaries and escape the confines of their job descriptions. Let's rescale our public services so that they are better able to support sustained learning relationships between public servants and communities. Small public services – that's a heresy for another day!

~

Catherine Needham is Professor of Public Policy and Public Management at the University of Birmingham. Her research focuses on two main areas:
- *adult social care (including care markets, personalisation, co-production, personal budgets)*
- *the public service workforce (roles, skills and values) and what it means to be a 21st-Century Public Servant and elected councillor.*

She has published a wide range of articles, chapters and books for academic and practitioner audiences. Her most recent book is Reimagining the Future Public Service Workforce *(Springer, 2019). She tweets as @DrCNeedham*

Bibliography

Asgarkhani, M. (2005) 'Digital government and its effectiveness in public management reform: A local government perspective', *Public Management Review.* 7(3) pp.465-487.

Bickerstaffe, S. (2013) *Towards Whole Person Care,* IPPR. http://bit.ly/kittens03

Clancy, G.P. & Duffy, F.D. (2013) 'Going "All In" to transform the Tulsa Community's health and health care workforce', *Academic Medicine.* 88(12), pp.1844-1848

Cooke, G. and Muir, R. (2012) *The Relational State,* Institute for Public Policy Research

Cottam, H. (2011) 'Relational Welfare', *Soundings,* (48), p.134.

Laloux, F. (2014) *Reinventing Organizations: A guide to creating organizations inspired by the next stage in human consciousness,* Nelson Parker

Davidson, C. (2011). 'So Last Century', *Times Higher Education,* 28, pp.32-36

Durose, C., Needham, C., Mangan, C. and Rees, J. (2017) 'Generating "good enough" evidence for co-production', *Evidence & Policy*, 13(1), pp.135-151.

Evans, T. (2016) *Professional discretion in welfare services: Beyond street-level bureaucracy*, Routledge

Exworthy, M. ed., (1998) *Professionals and New Managerialism*, McGraw-Hill Education

Fox, A. (2017) 'Bold academic decisions are required to support survival and transformation of social care sector', *University of Birmingham Perspective*, http://bit.ly/kittens05

Frank, R.G. (2013) 'Using Shared Savings to Foster Coordinated Care for Dual Eligible', *New England Journal of Medicine*. 368(5) pp.404-405

Glasby, J. (2014) 'The Controversies of Choice and Control: Why some people might be hostile to English social care reforms', *British Journal of Social Work*, 44(1) pp.252-266

Gray, B.H., Sarnak, J.S. & Burgers, J.S. (2015) *Case Study: Home care by self-governing nursing teams: The Netherlands' Buurtzorg model*, The Commonwealth Fund, www.commonwealthfund.org

Hochschild, A.R. (1983) *The Managed Heart: Commercialization of Human Feeling*, University of California Press

Hudson, B. (2015) 'Can GPs coordinate "whole person care"?' *Journal of Integrated Care*, 23(1), pp.10-16.

Kahana, E., Kelley-Moore, J. & Kahana, B. (2011) 'Proactive Aging: A longitudinal study of stress, resources, agency, and wellbeing in late life', *Aging & Mental Health*, 16(4) pp.438-451

Laragy, C., Fisher, K.R., Purcal, C. & Jenkinson, S. (2015) 'Australia's individualised disability funding packages: When do they provide greater choice and opportunity?' *Asian Social Work and Policy Review*, 9(3) pp.282-292

Lord, J. and Hutchison, P. (2003) 'Individualised support and funding: building blocks for capacity building and inclusion', *Disability & Society*, 18(1), pp.71-86

Morrell, K. (2007) 'Re-Defining Professions: Knowledge, Organization and Power as Syntax' (paper presented at the fifth annual Critical Management Studies Conference, University of Manchester, http://bit.ly/kittens01

Muir, R. and Parker, I. (2014). *Many to Many: How the relational state will transform public services*, IPPR

Needham, C., Mastracci, S. and Mangan, C. (2017) 'The Emotional Labour of Boundary Spanning', *Journal of Integrated Care*, 25(4), pp.288-300.

Needham, C. and Mangan, C. (2014) *The Twenty-First Century Public Servant*, University of Birmingham, available from http://bit.ly/kittens04

NHS England (2015) *Consensus Statement on Promoting Health and Wellbeing*, http://bit.ly/kittens02

Rittel, H.W. and Webber, M.M. (1973) 'Dilemmas in a General Theory of Planning', *Policy Sciences*, 4(2), pp.155-169.

Saks, M. (2013) 'Regulating the English healthcare professions: Zoos, circuses or safari parks?', *Journal of Professions and Organization*, 1(1), pp.84-98

Susskind, R. and Susskind, D. (2015) *The Future of the Professions: How technology will transform the work of human experts*, Oxford University Press

WHO: World Health Organization (2015) *WHO global strategy on people-centred and integrated health service*, World Health Organization

The Age of Impact: Why Charitable Giving Is Broken

Jake Hayman
CEO, Ten Years' Time

What is the orthodoxy you are challenging?

This chapter is about how a misguided obsession with impact is screwing up the charity sector.

There's an interesting exercise that you can do with a group of people – from billionaires to those on a minimum wage – that shows what I believe to be wrong with charitable giving. First, ask people to take a piece of paper and write on it three things:

1. the charity they give the most money to each year
2. the biggest problems they think the world is facing or their community is facing
3. what change needs to take place to make the world a better place.

What you will unfortunately but inevitably find is a frequent (if not universal) disconnect between the solutions people see as key, the problems that they believe we need to focus on and where they actually give.

For me, this discrepancy is the start of the problem. We have disaggregated that which we see to be important from those entities we give money to. It represents a fundamental lack of confidence in the ability of philanthropy to contribute to the changes we want to see in the world.

To understand how we fix it, we need to see how we got here, I believe there has been a logical, if misguided, journey through the world of 'impact'. In my romanticism I think of a time when charities were established based on a set of values and a determination to make a difference in the world and people funded them loyally.

A bygone era

I remember, when I was growing up, that I used to ask my grandparents if I could open their post. I was always fascinated by the charity appeals, the little envelopes asking us to fill them with coins that they would come and collect, the thank-you letters from the longstanding charities they supported making me proud of my generous grandparents.

It's 24 years since my last grandparent passed and no one in my direct family has started a direct debit to a charity since. I look around today at how money flows and it makes me profoundly sad. Maybe the charity sector that my grandparents knew was as deeply flawed as ours today, maybe the way they gave wasn't any better than the rest of us but there's something compelling about the idea that patiently and relentlessly supporting a set of values over time is as good a way as any to hope to change the world.

Has it all been turned upside down by short-termists in suits? In this chapter, I will set out how we got here and where we need to go next.

The four ages of impact

In **the first age of impact – the age of impact on the giver**, orthodoxy had it that people are selfish. This era was all about the manipulation of that selfishness to create an industry based only around the ego and self-worth of the philanthropist. Charity fundraisers realised that by selling feel-good, you could raise money: that people were interested in being thanked for the act of saving rather than bothered by issues of injustice.

Why fund grassroots community development when I can sell you this building with your name on it? Why fund lasting service improvement when you can see the joy in a homeless person's eyes when you save them from a night on the street? Why address structural inequality when you can fast-track one poor person to a job in a law firm via a scholarship education at Oxford and they will forever be in a debt of gratitude to you?

The Impact Era One philanthropists were sold a starting point that they were more than happy to believe: that society is fair and that they are its hardest workers. In this context, in doing good, they were deserving of gratitude even more than the poor were deserving of their good grace. They never started their philanthropic journey with the question about what really needed to change in the world.

They painted individuals, communities and, at their peak, an entire continent as needy and awaiting a saviour. The message was sold at such an industrial scale that we are still suffering from the prejudices that they perpetuated. They sold out the communities they should have been serving for a quick buck.

What did for Impact Era One was its own success. From tube stations to TV sets we were bombarded over and again with our opportunity to quite literally save the children. The donor was the active participant – it was our experience that mattered, while the child was simply a switch to be flicked from pathetic to grinning.

The business of selling became bigger and bigger but at some point took a step too far and moved from overdrive to meltdown. There were so many children to save at every bus stop and commercial break and so many charities saving them that it became a farce even to the people who had bought into it.

Something needed to change and change it did. In a response to the farce of the fundraisers, around twenty years ago a group of (predominantly) men left the City and decided to save us. In doing so, they brought the dawn of the **second age of impact, the age of measurement**. Despite what has come since, this remains the dominant age of philanthropic practice today as evidenced by the structures of application forms and grant reports across so many foundations.

The 'city boys' (closely followed by tech entrepreneurs and half of Oxford University) came with smart CVs, smart suits and tonnes of money. They had a couple of things holding them back. Firstly, they came with a fundamental suspicion of the charity sector – that it was inefficient and wasteful, that there were too many charities doing the same thing and that they were poorly run.

The second, even more importantly, was a collective ignorance of issues of inequality, service provision or basically any insight into the communities that we exist to serve.

Either way, they came and brought with them a simple answer to the problems of the charity sector: dump the soft stuff and show us the numbers.

Armed with annual impact reports and deeply flawed assessment tools, they started directing philanthropy away from fundraising campaigns and towards commissioning interventions based on spreadsheets. They began investing in programmes with a low cost per head and an expensive impact assessment being run by charities with hyper-efficient overheads.

Within a generation they had replaced what was left of the trust-based, values-aligned culture of giving that defined my grandparents' approach to charity with an approach that resembles active commissioning. SMART objectives, payments by results and harsh accountability were the future then. They transitioned out the soft charity trustees from the community and in came the professionals: lawyers, accountants and business leaders.

The problem was that they never stopped to ask what the purpose of philanthropy was.

I believe that the purpose of philanthropy is not to replicate or expand government expenditure, but to do what government is bad at: to build community, to take a long-term view that isn't constrained by departmental structures, top-down approaches or electoral cycles. It is our opportunity to think, reflect and create space that isn't dictated by the command and control of wealthy white men.

Of course, data matters and, if only we were gathering it to learn rather than to congratulate ourselves, we might actually get somewhere. If only we were looking over ten-year horizons rather than ten-month ones, we might actually make a difference. But we aren't and we don't and so here we landed.

Anyway, none of those failures mattered to the Age of Measurement. It was an age that ultimately made a rod for its own back when, by its own numbers, it came to understand that it wasn't actually achieving very much.

It had made sense that we would want to spend money on better programmes over worse programmes and have higher social return on investment rather than lower, but we weren't achieving scale. Somewhere, somehow, and without any sense of irony, the City folk forgot to run the numbers and realise that philanthropic pockets simply weren't deep enough to deliver services at scale – that being efficient and effective with their next hundred grand made not a bit of difference to the bigger picture. A new approach was needed and from this moment of enlightenment was born the **third age of impact: the age of organisational impact.**

We had the answers but they weren't leading to change at scale. So it was decided that we needed a new financing model that wasn't based on philanthropy. Having learnt very little from our Second Age, we turned again away from communities, specialists and frontline workers and looked instead to venture capitalists to provide our inspiration.

We decided that market forces were the only way to achieve lasting scale and so we needed to move away from relying on the good will of philanthropists and small-scale donors alike. We needed investment.

Wherever possible we scrapped anything that would need long-term philanthropic funding from our consciousness and left those causes penniless. In their place, we flooded cash into anything shiny that had a revenue model behind it, regardless of whether it was of any real use to anyone. COOs and professional boards became the name of the game and its key players were charismatic 'social entrepreneurs'.

The impact we were seeking had moved from the giver to the beneficiary and now to the organisation itself: how could we get it 'investment ready', how could we get it performance-by-results contracts, how could we get it to trade for its income? The buzzwords of innovation, scale and sustainability were the only ones that mattered.

The social finance folk have a great story about putting fences at the top of a cliff rather than sending ambulances to pick up bodies at the bottom of it and how much money it saves – what a great social enterprise clifftop fences are. But who are these people toppling off cliffs? People aren't idiots. If I was near a dangerous cliff edge no fucking way am I going near it. If you have an epidemic of bodies at the bottom of a cliff then for me you either have a serious drug and/or alcohol problem that is affecting people's judgement, a mental health and wellbeing problem that is leading to suicides, high winds coming from climate change or a maniac on the loose pushing people off a cliff face.

In any instance, your fence brings down your bills for body collections but it doesn't affect your addiction, mental health, crime or climate problems. So the killer goes to lie in wait somewhere else.

At its best, social investment has done a lot of good. It has brought investment in community business and products tailored to those communities that mainstream business left behind. It has encouraged new SMEs to think about accounting for social and ecological as well as financial values and it has brought new money, some brilliant people and some great ideas. It has put the question of whether or not it makes sense for a foundation that has an endowment invested in coal, oil, gas, sugar, porn, arms and tobacco to have a registered charitable status at all. At its best it's done a lot of good.

At its worse though, this age was hijacked by people whose only thought is how we get a fiscal 'exit' from the sustainable fence-building company. The board meetings at such companies transformed from being about challenges the community faced to being about solutions to pursue then to being about how to legally prevent anyone else from using fences as a suicide prevention tool in order to protect our investment.

The term 'fiduciary duty' became more and more prominent in social purpose organisations and the line between the hedge-funders who buy pharmaceuticals patents and make medicine unaffordable and the rest of us became blurred. Success rather than morality became the key distinguishing factor between charitable enterprise and the worst of capitalism. To the horror of those who wanted the best for this age, our soul got left at the door and the communities we served didn't even know which doors decisions about their lives were getting made behind any more. Charities became more and more obsessed with growth and the remaining community board members were replaced by aggressive marketeers and commercial investors.

What did for the hype of the third age was the awakening realisation that a world of great sustainable social enterprises looked much like the world without them. We came to realise that ideas that would challenge the status quo had no market within it. When it came to anything important, the system wasn't interested to buy the best of what we as a sector were selling.

And so came the **fourth age of impact: the age of systems and place.** The opening of our eyes to the fact that the systems we sought to affect were wholly unfit for the purpose we believed them to be serving. We needed to help them be stronger so that they could make better decisions.

Why was it that a 'high impact' drug and alcohol rehabilitation programme delivered by a sustainable scalable social enterprise wasn't working? Because it was undermined by the fact that a decent proportion of the people using it were out of work and/or living on the streets and/or suffering from mental health problems and trauma. Everything was made worse by the various arms of government not working together to provide its services in synch. Vulnerable people were 'done to' and endlessly intervened upon and selling more interventions was never going to fix that. Programmes weren't working because the system was set up in a way that made their failure inevitable.

And so people started trying to work to share data and organise collaboratively across public, private and social ecosystems and within geographies. We realised that rather than simply dump malaria nets one month, vaccines the next and de-worming drugs the next... and expect everyone to be well, it might be worth thinking about supporting a strong locally-led infrastructure for health delivery and monitoring.

Domestically is has taken us a lot longer to realise that all the work we do is part of a complex ecosystem and that poor people are equally complex and no more 'fixable' than rich people. We came to realise that we couldn't continue to deliver programmes in spite of the system and instead that we might want to start to get it functioning better as a whole.

The Age of Systems and Place is all about making the ecosystem that we are a part of stronger, more joined up. It brings professional development programmes and recruitment programmes for frontline workers, accountability infrastructure, 'joined-up thinking', data-sharing, multi-agency taskforces and so on.

If we could just get these services to work a little better together, to be a bit more effective, to join up, we could create great societies through the most strategic of philanthropic gifts.

The problem, of course, is that every system is perfectly designed to create the outcomes it creates. We assume that this perfect design is accidental but it isn't, it is very, very purposeful. Why was it that charities and social enterprises weren't making a difference to re-offending rates in the criminal justice system? Why is it that, when we then strengthened this system through investing in it, things didn't get any better either? Because the system is set up to punish not to prevent reoffending. We were strengthening systems that are designed to be regressive.

Domestically and internationally we have come to realise that systems strengthening is welcomed by those we wish to work with but system reform far less so. In a practical sense we were too often left strengthening systems that we didn't believe in.

As much as you can criticise, these ages have generally been led by people desperate to make things better and each still has a huge amount to offer. At different times I have worked in service of each of them. They have all had the same common problem though – that they were defined, designed and pioneered by privileged white men. I cannot think of a single major foundation board that is largely made up of the communities that it exists to serve. I cannot think of a single philanthropist who has fully devolved their philanthropy to communities and frontline workers rather than decided on their behalf.

Foundation boardrooms are full of the privileged. Staff teams too often are too. The charities we serve have noticed that foundations and philanthropists like to see boards of professionals and so have migrated them in and migrated everyone else out. In turn those charity boards have then appointed people from professional backgrounds into their leadership teams and we have created layer after layer of hierarchy where the voice of the communities we serve is at best a minority and at worst non-existent. Looking at government, things are often no different.

So what can we hope for in the future? Well we hope we will look back on the Age of Measurement and thank it for giving us the tools to learn and prioritise. We will hope to look back on the Age of Organisational Impact and thank it for giving us the tools to release money spent in emergencies into work that is preventative, that it will have helped us think through organisational models that can serve social change, that it will have shamed us into dumping our endowment advisors for more progressive ones and that it will have required mainstream business to be more social. We will look back on the Age of Systems and thank it for forcing us to accept complexity and we will look back at grandma and thank her for teaching us about the importance of values and long-termism.

What has to change and who has to change it?

But all of this will remain insufficient unless we embrace the charity sector in our **fifth age of impact: the age of power.** We are starting to hear those conversations that many thinkers in this space have been having for decades at last enter the conferences and board rooms of philanthropy. The reason that disadvantage exists in our country is because we rigged it to be that way – from our education system to our housing, our employment practices to our social care, our corporate regulation to our taxation. All are shaped in rooms by people who are disproportionately from the same small sub-section of society that were in those rooms a generation ago and a generation before that and indeed, ten generations before that. They all believe in an economic paradigm of trickle-down that says look after the rich and everyone else will be fine. It is, of course, nonsense.

The fifth age of impact is about power and voice: not about 'giving' anyone a voice but about philanthropists and foundations working to circumvent the layers and layers of mufflers that currently prevent community voices from ever being heard.

The fifth age, if successful, will see a reclaiming of the charity sector and all the various programmatic and funding organisations that make it up by the communities it exists to serve.

It will become about new narratives surrounding power and voice, citizenship, belonging, rights and responsibilities and fairness that are for the first time led not by a conservative minority but instead by a grassroots majority. It is an age where the philanthropist is a servant of the community, not the other way around.

~

Jake Hayman is the CEO of philanthropy education firm, Ten Years' Time, which he started following a semi-professional poker career. He has spent his career starting new social enterprises and creative businesses. In 2008 he founded social enterprise 'Future First' to build alumni networks in public high schools across the UK and is now taking the model around the world. Jake sits on the trustee boards of the Early Intervention Foundation and the £100m Lankelly Chase Foundation and is a course tutor for the University of Cambridge course on corporate philanthropy.

The Organisation is Dead – Long Live the Network

Stephen Lock

Head of Business Intelligence, National Institute for Health Research Clinical Research Network

The orthodoxy I am challenging

If something big needs to be done, if some great undertaking must be begun, if many people must be rallied to a single cause, what kind of structure do we imagine to accomplish the task? For the most part, we imagine some kind of formal organisation. This might be a company, a university, a military unit, a government department or a trust.

Despite their very different purposes, something that each of these organisations shares is that they are, by nature, hierarchical. Each will have a single leader or figurehead, possibly some kind of board, and then layers of management controlling ever more junior members of staff.

It is a belief in the need for control, which justifies and sustains the idea that organisations are necessary and, to a large extent, the natural order in human endeavour. In truth, this idea is no longer relevant in the modern world, but we have yet to fully see through the falsehoods of the orthodoxy, nor to grasp the potential of the alternative. But the truth is: *the organisation is dead – long live the network.* We can all agree that, right?

Of course we can't. Plenty of arguments have been made for a change in management structure. You might want an agile team or a self-organising squad or a maybe your organisation needs a tribe? In short, if you want a justification for changing your organisation into something that can squeeze as much juice for its shareholders or a government department as possible, you can find lots to work with on the bookshelves of any business school.

So, what's wrong with that? These are just more ways of organising organisations. But none of them offers the fundamental change that its proponents claim. While systems like this may reduce hierarchy somewhat, they also have their own forms of leverage. No self-respecting agile development company can exist without a unit of 'SCRUM Masters' to make sure they keep everyone under just enough control.

My heresy

Everyone believes in the need to control others through an organisation to some extent. We've all been convinced that without hierarchy and control, there would be chaos and, therefore, we must step into line. This tendency seems to exert itself more in people when they are given control. Endow somebody with a job title like 'manager', 'director' or 'policy maker' and that's what they will do. Moreover, the structures around them are likely to bombard them with controlling messages in the form of performance targets and red, amber, green charts, making it hard for them to stop creating more hierarchy in a desperate attempt to gain more control.

What if we could rip all that up, even in the public sector? What if we could move the centre of our focus away from the organisation and towards the individual as part of a community? And yet still get stuff done, still serve citizens or customers or, heaven forbid, fellow humans?

That might be a much more satisfying world to live and work in, don't you think? We just need to convince managers, directors and policy makers that the way they see the world of work is fundamentally wrong.

What the world needs is less control, less hierarchy and more, genuine networking. So my heresy is that *the organisation, as we know it, is dead.*

Where is the current orthodoxy held and who holds it?

When discussing an orthodoxy, it is important to understand where it comes from. That way one can take up a position to counter the existing arguments. But, in this case, the orthodoxy is held by almost all of us. It is ingrained. It is something we are conditioned to think, as were our mothers and fathers down the generations. But why?

Perhaps it is because the people with the power want us to think this way. And we want to believe that, by handing over control, we'll be protected by the structures around (or above) us. And the nub of the problem, but also the solution, rests with those two words: power and control.

What's wrong with the current orthodoxy?

What would happen if we tried to achieve substantial change in our chosen field or area of interest without creating a structure where power was granted from the top down and where nobody sought to control anybody else? Would it be chaotic? Would it struggle without strong leadership? Would anything ever get done?

While these are natural questions to ask, they are the wrong ones. Perhaps we should be asking ourselves what kinds of relationships, values and goals we would like to share with other people. We could then seek to come together in a way that meets our instinctive human desires to be valued, to be equal, to be able to contribute and to achieve a common purpose.

So why don't we? In part because we've always (or we think we've always) done things this way. It is in the interests of people who hold power to impose hierarchy and to try to control those with less power. Not because it creates better outcomes, but because it maintains their status.

And those without power believe it is in their interests to back people who embody power and hierarchy because of the propaganda of the powerful. See how a lack of government consensus over complex issues is routinely characterised as weakness. Following any path determinedly (however unclear the evidence) is seen as strength.

So why do we think like this? Intellectually, it can be traced at least as far back as Plato, who contended that governing structures would always move through five regimes (Aristocracy, Timocracy, Oligarchy, Democracy and Tyranny) with an inevitable, progressive degeneration towards Tyranny. Therefore, he concluded, power must be seized to maintain order.

Plato contended that power should be held by a caste of philosopher kings, rather like, well, Plato. So the priests of philosophy, religion, war or Wall Street want it that way. After all, it's their way. And they have done a damn fine job of convincing us all that it is the only way.

What needs to change and who has to change it?

If it was ever so, why should it change now? The short answer is technology, particularly social media (more of that later), artificial intelligence (AI) and robotics.

A report by PwC (*UK Economic Outlook: Prospects for the economy, the productivity challenge and migration after Brexit, November 2017*) found that 30% of jobs were at high risk of automation as a result of AI and robotics. "PwC said 2.25 million jobs were at high risk in wholesale and retailing – the sector that employs most people in the UK – and 1.2 million were under threat in manufacturing, 1.1 million in administrative and support services and 950,000 in transport and storage."[1]

However, it isn't just traditionally working-class jobs that are at risk. Many studies of the potential of AI suggest that roles such as para-legals and computer programmers are also at high risk of automation. Very few organisations are immune.

Most commentators, faced with this kind of prediction, focus (legitimately) on the effects on the people and communities that might be impacted. But few consider what will happen to the organisations that currently employ them. What happens when a large law firm automates all of its para-legal work? Clearly, at some point you will no longer need a para-legal team, but will you need administrators and accountants to support them? Will you need buildings for them to work in, which need to be cleaned and maintained? Will you need trainers to train them and managers to manage them?

The answer is no. So when an organisation is hollowed out by automation, what is left? And is there anything the people affected can do to protect themselves?

Take teaching, for example. Although teaching is considered to be at low risk of automation, the advent of MOOCs (massive open online courses) means that many adults can be educated at home, or in Starbucks, without ever needing to set foot in a university. If enough people decide they can learn what they need to learn, in small pieces, from the likes of LearnDirect or the Kahn Academy, what will happen to the fee structures of the universities? What will happen to all the ancillary functions and the estates of a university if the money from students dries up?

The same could also be true of healthcare. In the UK we take for granted the National Health Service (NHS) and revere it so much we put it at the heart of the 2012 Olympic Games opening ceremony. No politician could last more than a few days if they ever proposed tampering with a model that delivers healthcare free at the point of need.

But what if the threat to the NHS was from automation and technology, rather than politics? There is already a wide range of systems and technologies that can diagnose disease better than humans. It is far easier to arrange a consultation via Skype than to attend in person. If enough people

---

[1] Larry Elliott, economics editor, writing in *The Guardian*, 'Robots', 24 Mar 2017.

choose new ways of diagnosing and consulting outside of the established model of care, will there be sufficient skill and resource remaining in the NHS to sustain the kind of top-down delivery of services we have become accustomed to?

What's the solution to a collapsing hierarchy?

If a seismic change is on the horizon and if organisations and established hierarchies are collapsing, perhaps we can no longer sustain the idea that we should subordinate our needs to those of the powerful in return for protection. So what can we do instead? The answer is in front of us already. To see this more clearly, try a little thought experiment:

1. Imagine that project you wish you could get around to
2. Mentally assemble your dream team of collaborators
3. Then, ask yourself, what proportion of them sit in the same office as you?

In all likelihood the answer to No. 3 is very few. If you were assembling your dream team of collaborators, you would reach out to your network of contacts, friends and associates. Maybe you would ask somebody you admire to act as a mentor. You wouldn't just consider who happened to be in close physical proximity, from nine till five, Monday to Friday.

So, perhaps it is time to ask yourself, what makes you effective when you work? Is it the building you work in? The payroll and personnel departments? The managers above you? Or your network of humans?

In order to rid ourselves of the belief that hierarchy is important, we need to recognise the true power of the social and professional networks we inhabit. We need to recognise that we all belong to networks, but, more than that, we need to understand what they are and how they work. Then we need to actively build and promote them.

What is a network?

The public sector in the UK is already leading the way in the development of serious, professional networks, particularly in healthcare. For example, the National Institute of Health Research Clinical Research Network (NIHR CRN) is probably the largest research delivery organisation in the world, linking together every healthcare provider in the country. It achieves this by linking people together to work towards a common purpose, to improve the health and wealth of the nation.

Professor Becky Malby has conducted several reviews of networks in healthcare. She writes[2] that "Networks are often creative, innovative places where resources can be shared for the common good. They are highly relevant at a time when resource is under pressure and when long-established working patterns have to change."

Similarly, Susannah Randall writes[3] that "Networks are defined as cooperative structures where an interconnected group, or system, coalesce around shared purpose, and where members act as peers on the basis of reciprocity and exchange, based on trust, respect and mutuality."

Why wouldn't any of us want more of that?

The question of leadership

One defining difference between a network and a traditional organisation lies in the nature of leadership. Leadership needs to adapt in this new model of working. Network leaders need to remind themselves constantly that 'it's not about me'. It's about diversity, connections, strong relationships, learning from experiences, common understanding, equality and sharing. It's not about great men, institutionalisation, control, governance and bureaucracy, winners and losers, or special interests. As Binney et al write[4], "To hell with great men... Leading happens between people".

To help with this process we have some powerful, positive technologies. Social media tools such as Facebook and Twitter enable the rapid development of non-hierarchical networks. The ability to create large, secure groups through technology like WhatsApp allows people to have conversations safely across continents. This makes it incredibly easy for people to develop reciprocal relationships around a common purpose. What's more, these networks can adapt in order to thrive, with distributed leadership models ensuring that knowledge is drawn from a diverse range of people.

---

[2] Becky Malby, Professor of Health Systems Innovation, Health Systems Innovation Lab, London South Bank University

[3] *Learning report: Leading networks in healthcare.* The Health Foundation, 2013

[4] Binney, George, Williams, Colin and Wilke, Gerhard (2012) *Living Leadership: A Practical Guide for Ordinary Heroes,* 3rd ed. FT Publishing International

Enrique Mendizabal defines[5] six main functions for networks:

- Filter – Decide what is worth paying attention to
- Amplify – Make ideas more widely understood
- Invest/provide – Give resources to members
- Convene – Bring people together
- Build communities – Promote and sustain values and standards
- Facilitate – Help members carry out activities more effectively.

We can build on the functions of networks to consider their effects – one of which is that they can expand rapidly and widely, because their members benefit from adding new links and, as a consequence, they generally seek to make new connections. As they do this, the network gains capacity to diffuse information and resources more and more widely. This diffusion effect allows networks to spread ideas and generate feedback rapidly.

Plastrik et al describe[6] the idea of "Small World" reach, where networks can bring people together efficiently and in novel combinations, because they provide remarkably short pathways between individuals separated by geographic or social distance. Also, bridges are easily built across social and physical barriers because of the common purpose the members share. Once built, these bridges are available to other members of the network, enabling a few short hops to collaboration.

Other key features of networks are that they are adaptive and resilient. Links can be created between people with relative ease. If members choose to leave the network, it does not unduly affect the ability of the network as a whole to continue to function. Similarly, links in a network can be latent for a long time, with people not actively participating. And then, as an issue of interest spreads across the links in the network, those links can fire up, releasing capacity as it is needed.

Contrast these functions and effects of networks with those of a traditional, hierarchical organisation. Are they resilient, if a significant senior manager leaves? Can they adapt to breaks in communication up and down the chain of command? Are they comfortable with latency; with members of the hierarchy not participating until they can add value? Do

---

[5] Mendizabal, E. (2006) *Understanding networks: the functions of research policy networks*, Working Paper 271. London: Overseas Development Institute.

[6] Plastrik, P. and Taylor, M. (2006) *Net gains: A handbook for network builders seeking social change*. Wendling Foundation, http://bit.ly/kittens13

they grow organically, or does growth have to be directed and pre-planned? Are they good at convening people and building communities?

It is this rigidity and lack of vitality in the structures of traditional organisations that will make them increasingly unsustainable. And as they die, networks will take their place.

Organisations and Hierarchies Have Their Place

There are times and situations where a traditional hierarchy might be more appropriate than a network, such as:

- If the problem is simple, it is better to just get on with it rather than to discuss it
- If decision-making can't be shared, it would be unfair to simulate consultation
- If funding must be tightly controlled, then tight reins might be appropriate
- If you need repetition, rather than creativity, simple control structures will work.

However, if you want to have resilience to overcome the rapid changes in employment we expect over the coming decades, you should put your faith in a network of humans to support you, rather than the organisation that currently pays your salary.

So, why not build your own network?

The beauty of networks is that you can belong to as many, or as few as you like. In fact, when you think about it, you are already a member of lots of informal (e.g. a Facebook interest group) or semi-formal (e.g. a local choir) networks. You just need to acknowledge how important they are, and work at making them a central, rather than a peripheral, part of your experience.

You don't need your superior's permission to join or even form a network. And the moment you do, you instantly increase your access to support, opportunities, inspiration and ideas. You will benefit from diversity, passion and interest from across the globe.

A lesson from history

We think we know that hierarchies are the natural way to organise people. We think we know that this is how things have always been. But, in part, this is because of the distorted view of history that celebrates great men and great deeds and great events over an understanding of how humans support one another – be that through the foundation of the Union Movement in 18th-century Britain, or the #metoo campaign, which started in 21st-century America. And there is one part of the world where this tradition runs deeper.

Oscar Guardiola-Rivera tells the tale[7] of William Denevan, Professor Emeritus of Geography at the University of Wisconsin-Madison. In 1961, Prof Denevan first flew over the region of Beni in Bolivia. This is a remote and difficult area of the Amazon basin that is desert for half the year and flooded by snow melt for the other half.

As he looked down, he saw straight lines running for thousands of miles across this landscape. Straight lines that could not have been created by nature. Over many years of study, archaeologists subsequently discovered that the entire region is anthropogenic, that those straight lines were man-made transportation canals and causeways linking hundreds of elevated mounds. Each of these small mounds supported a village that worked with neighbouring villages to maintain the canals and causeways so that the land could be managed and farmed. And they did this 3-5,000 years ago.

What Professor Denevan had discovered was one of the most remarkable human achievements on the continent. And yet it took almost four decades for this discovery to be believed, with people suggesting all kinds of irrational causes of the straight lines, ditches and mounds.

It took so long because the "Earthmovers of the Amazon" left no evidence of kings or top-down control. As the prevailing orthodoxy states that humans can only achieve things on this scale if they are commanded to do so by a great man, it has taken a shift in mindset to understand what humans have always been able to achieve if they build networks and collaborate.

The truth is, if people build a network, they can literally change the landscape.

~

Stephen Lock is the Head of Business Intelligence at the National Institute for Health Research Clinical Research Network.

---

[7] Guardiola-Rivera, Oscar (2011) *What if Latin America Ruled the World? How the South Will Take the North into the 22nd Century.* Bloomsbury

Evidence isn't Enough

Peter Wright
Convenor, North East Public Health SkunkWorks

In about 2008, some people in the field of public health did some excellent research into the impact of imposing a minimum unit price on alcohol. The research was impeccable, and their findings were professionally presented. From a public health perspective, the case for a minimum unit price was watertight – it is a highly effective measure in helping a small group of problem drinkers significantly improve control over their drinking.

In late 2012, the government consulted on some potential policies to cut alcohol-related crime and antisocial behaviour. One of the potential measures was the introduction of a minimum price per unit of alcohol.

In her response to the results of the consultation, the then Home Secretary Theresa May said that consultation responses had "not provided evidence that conclusively demonstrates that Minimum Unit Pricing (MUP) will actually do what it is meant to: reduce problem drinking without penalising all those who drink responsibly."

Because the very professional and well-presented evidence in support of the measure didn't convince the Home Secretary in 2012, nothing happened. Each year since then, around 960 people have died unnecessarily in the UK, and we've lost around £5bn/year to NHS, crime and absence costs that the measure would have prevented. This example shows that being *too* professional with evidence has a human, financial and societal cost.

What is the orthodoxy I am challenging?

The current orthodoxy is that professional well-presented evidence is enough. In this chapter, I argue that this is naïve and unrealistic, and things are getting harder, much harder. In this context, the Collins Dictionary 'word of 2017' was the term 'fake news'.

Most of the experiences that have led to this heresy have come through my work in local government and wider public health, including working on the development and introduction of the 2007 smoke-free legislation, dealing with policy on alcohol, and a collaboration with Durham University on conspiracy theories and health[1].

I learned a lot from a session delivered to a Faculty of Public Health conference by the Public Health Minister of the time. The minister warned delegates that "pure" public health evidence had little power in the melee of brokering changes to public policy in Cabinet and other parliamentary fora. The argument that 'This measure will save lives' competed on an equal footing with 'This measure will lose tax revenue' and carried considerably less weight than 'This measure will lose us votes'. The minister implored delegates to provide their evidence in a far more influential manner than before, if we wanted to see the changes we sought.

Who holds it?

We have a whole industry creating great evidence, and this should be the foundation of excellent public policy. Largely this is in academia, but the evidence industry isn't restricted to academics.

What exactly is 'evidence'?

As I get older I increasingly hold the belief that everyone should carry, and use, a pocket dictionary.

I frequently see the impact of people agreeing to do things that will fail to materialise, simply because of some basic differences in how key words are understood in different spheres of work. Agreements are made, but people find later that they hadn't actually agreed to the same thing.

Indeed, the whole nation took a vote in 2016 over Europe, and it has since become clear that there was never a common understanding in voters' minds exactly what 'leaving the European Union' actually meant.

---

[1] Conspiracy Theories in Health Special Interest Group:
https://www.dur.ac.uk/wolfson.institute/sig/conspiracy/

There are several definitions of the word 'evidence' so from here I'll stick to the Dictionary.com version:

> that which tends to prove or disprove something; ground for belief; proof.

Much of my early career involved taking cases to court and proving things 'beyond reasonable doubt'. I've needed to have sufficient confidence in my evidence to take an oath to tell the truth and be aggressively cross-examined by someone paid to create doubt.

Policy makers don't like doubt. If I achieve nothing else in this chapter, I need the reader to understand and accept that doubt is the enemy of the evidence holder. If we aren't confident in our evidence, able to explain it in layperson's terms, and passionate about it being the foundation of policy, why would any policy maker act on it?

What is your heresy?

Only a small number of people within the evidence industry are capable of effectively using evidence to influence public policy. Most of the evidence is wasted and this comes at a huge cost. My heresy is that, in creating great public policy, *evidence isn't enough.*

We understand that individual decisions made by ordinary people will often be based on bias, preconceived ideas, a desire to fit in, and many other factors. We're used to people making seemingly bizarre life choices with dire consequences – people who smoke understand that it is terrible for their health, and people who gamble understand that they'll always lose in the end.

Individuals are fallible, but we hope that governments, public bodies and public servants will make better decisions than we do. We would like to believe that all decisions made in the interests of the public will be based on good evidence, sound reasoning and logic. But they aren't.

People are often surprised to find that much public policy is the result of the same flawed decision-making process that individuals may use, and important policy decisions can be made that impact on people's lives just as negatively as a personal decision to smoke or to gamble.

We accept that, sometimes, flawed public policy is inevitable, particularly when it is based on strong political dogma or detailed manifesto pledges.

But much of the time it should be possible for well presented evidence to form the basis of a sound decision, yet still something goes wrong.

What does go wrong?

Simplistically, public policy is made by politicians, by public servants or, occasionally, by the public.

People make policy, and people are complex, subject to all forms of bias and prejudice and, most important, fallible. Mistakes can be made, and this is part of life. But what prevents a lot of evidence turning into the basis of public policy is beyond these simple human failings; it is a problem with people.

1. Human failings – Policy makers are people, what could possibly go wrong?

> Policy makers are time-poor and stressed, so they ignore evidence that is difficult to interpret quickly.

I picked up this excellent quote from Luke Craven at his 'Little Heresies' presentation in 2016. Helping time-poor and stressed policy makers to have evidence that is easy to interpret must become one of the main priorities for evidence holders.

Most of us don't like presenting our evidence in a form that is easy to understand. Richard Smith, a former *BMJ* editor has complained that[2]:

> Too often, academic journals are filled with complex language and turgid prose, which is intended not to inform the reader but to ennoble the writer.

We can be reticent about using short words and short sentences. Plain English seems simplistic and unprofessional. Short is bad.

This is *our* problem, and we need to be willing to deal with it. If your work, and your evidence, is trivial then it really doesn't matter if you decide not to communicate it effectively to a policy maker. But what if it actually is important, possibly a matter of life and death? In such cases I'd argue that your professionalism and your pride must come second to influencing the policy makers who you need to turn your evidence into policy.

In 2008, I witnessed a very senior local politician asking a very well qualified Public Health professional what would be the best thing that could be done to help improve health in his constituency. The Public Health professional chose to summarise the massive wisdom she carried around in her head in two words, "tackle smoking". For years after this encounter, the politician was a phenomenal advocate for tackling smoking in both his constituency and in parliament. In this case, short was good.

---

[2] Richard Smith's BMJ Blog: http://bit.ly/turgidprose

We're all subject to bias. In his *Cognitive Biases Codex*[3], John Manoogian III clusters about 190 individual forms of cognitive bias into 20 categories, and these 20 categories are further grouped into 4 larger groupings:

- What should we remember?
- Need to act fast
- Too much information
- Too little meaning.

Cognitive biases are our way of attempting to find meaning in the complexity of our lives, a way of filtering a massive array of data and information so that we can make use of it, or ignore it.

Our biases and our belief systems develop over a lifetime. It is rare that a single piece of killer evidence can totally transform how we think. Few evidence holders have the time or resources to mount a long-term campaign of educating, drip feeding and correcting misunderstandings in order to have their evidence understood, accepted and trusted.

One of the 190 cognitive biases, Illusory Superiority, is particularly important to how confident an evidence holder might seem to a policy maker.

> In the modern world the stupid are cocksure while the intelligent are full of doubt.

Bertrand Russell said this in 1933 in 'The Triumph of Stupidity'. He was preceded in expressing this view by Confucius, Socrates, Shakespeare, Darwin and Yeats. This concept was later academically researched by Dunning and Kruger, whose work[4] was published in 1999 (and awarded an Ig Nobel Prize for Psychology in 2000).

Those in possession of an excellent grasp of the facts are often less confident in their knowledge than those with little or no knowledge. Whilst this sounds counterintuitive, its effects can be regularly seen in discussions about climate change, vaccination and in most areas of wider public policy.

In early 2016, when I started to prepare my talk in the 'Little Heresies' series on which this chapter is based, some of the problems I was going to talk about were not that widely recognised. Then we had the Referendum on Europe and the Presidential Election in the USA, and the world seemed to change. In 2019, the firm belief of large portions of the population in manufactured lies is becoming a major issue, and in some quarters it is

---

[3] http://bit.ly/cognitivebiasescodex

[4] Dunning and Kruger Effect: http://bit.ly/krugeranddunning

becoming acceptable to consider that a firmly held belief carries the same weight as a scientifically proven fact.

As long ago as 2008, Dr Ben Goldacre wrote in his book, *Bad Science*, that

> Without anybody noticing, bullshit has become an extremely important public health issue.

In a world that is tired of experts[5], turning good evidence into good public policy has suddenly become a lot harder than ever before. I will conclude my description of human failings with an 18th-century quote from Jonathan Swift: "It is useless to attempt to reason a man out of a thing he was never reasoned into".

2. Business interests – the influence of power, agnotology and denialism, and the effects of regulatory capture

About two centuries after Swift, Pulitzer Prize winner Upton Sinclair wrote

> It is difficult to get a man to understand something, when his salary depends upon his not understanding it!

This is a very appropriate thought with which to start this section on the deliberate creation of misinformation and manufactured confusion. Agnotology is the study of wilful acts to spread confusion and deceit, usually to sell a product or win favour.

As 'ologies' go, it isn't a well-known one. It goes hand in hand with other terminology with which only a few will be familiar; including Sockpuppets, Shills, Strawmen and Astroturfing. I'll let you look these up, as there isn't space in this chapter, but I should define the overarching concept used to create such confusion – Denialism[6]. The Hoofnangle brothers define it[7] thus:

> the employment of rhetorical arguments to give the appearance of legitimate debate where there is none, an approach that has the ultimate goal of rejecting a proposition on which a scientific consensus exists.

---

[5] Have we fallen out of love with experts? http://bit.ly/doesheknowwhatitslikeinsainsburys

[6] Denialism (academic version): http://bit.ly/denalismforacademics; (lay version) http://bit.ly/Denialismforlaypeople

[7] http://scienceblogs.com/denialism/about.php

There is a tight scientific consensus on manmade climate change, smoking causing cancer and vaccines being great at preventing certain diseases, but there is also a massive amount of manufactured doubt.

> Doubt is our product, since it is the best means of competing with the 'body of fact' that exists in the mind of the general public. It is also the means of establishing a controversy.[8]

Although it is widely reported that the techniques involved in denialism were created in the tobacco industry in the early 1990s, some scholars believe that it has earlier roots in the motor industry. Whatever the source, denialist techniques have been used by the motor, tobacco, food, drink and firearms industries for several decades to impede the creation of laws and restrictions that would protect the public from the harm caused by their products and lead to restricted sales.[9]

Denialism is a useful tool for anyone interested in stopping the creation of public policy. 'Regulatory Capture' is the ultimate goal for a business lobbyist wanting to protect his employer from unwanted state interference.

> When regulatory capture occurs, the interests of firms or political groups are prioritized over the interests of the public, leading to a net loss for society. [10]

Denialism in action – back to minimum unit price for alcohol

Around 2007, the Chief Medical Officer expressed some interest in the concept of minimum unit price for alcohol. This measure is used in some other countries and is very effective in reducing one form of alcohol harm – regular and excessive consumption of cheap alcohol by alcoholics who are unable to work. It has little or no impact on other alcohol-related problems, and none of its proponents had ever made such claims.

By 2011, corporate lobbyists had done such a good job of instilling mistaken beliefs about the purpose of a minimum unit price, that the Health Secretary trotted out around a dozen strawmen in an interview. A strawman is an irrelevant argument that takes debate away from the issue in question. The ice cream scene[11] from 'Thank you for Smoking' illustrates this.

---

[8] Brown & Williamson Tobacco Corp. Smoking and Health Proposal 1969

[9] ASH UK – early tobacco denialism: http://bit.ly/Smokefilledroom; later tobacco denialism: http://bit.ly/Tobacconomics

[10] Regulatory Capture: https://en.wikipedia.org/wiki/Regulatory_capture

[11] http://bit.ly/theicecreamscene

Mr Lansley's Straw Men[12]

The Health Secretary says there are "big problems" with the idea, which would penalise the poor, fall foul of EU competition laws, and do little to tackle the kind of dangerous drinking seen in town and city centres on Friday and Saturday nights. Mr Lansley told *The Independent on Sunday*:

"Are we really saying that because a bottle of vodka isn't £8 but £12.50 they are not going to preload with a bottle of vodka for a night out when they are in clubs where they pay £5 for a drink? That is absurd. They are still going to do this binge drinking because that is a behaviour issue. We have got to do much more to focus on what this means."

The Health Secretary conceded that higher prices for drink can reduce consumption but added: *"It is more likely to have a bigger proportionate impact on responsible drinkers who happen to be low-income households."*

His rejection of the idea will lay the Government open to claims that it has sided with big business, but Mr Lansley argues that a minimum price of 50p per unit would hand £600m in extra revenue to drinks firms. He maintains that the causes of binge drinking are too complex to be solved simply by raising prices.

"The cost of alcohol in Britain is the same in different parts," he said.

"But we have got lots of women in the North East who are fetching up in critical units with chronic alcohol abuse and liver disease on a regular basis – far more than in Hampshire. There are disparities that are nothing to do with price. We need to be realistic about what it is we are trying to address, which isn't simply if you raise the price all our problems will go away.

The question is, what is the relationship between price changes and alcohol misuse? Because alcohol consumption and alcohol misuse are not on a straight line to each other."

The alcohol strategy is expected to bolster Mr Lansley's concept of community alcohol partnerships, where police, retailers and trading standards unite to crackdown on underage drinking and booze-fuelled antisocial behaviour. Mr Lansley added:

""I think we can do immensely better in terms of preventing sales to youngsters."

---

[12] Independent Article on Minimum Unit Price: http://bit.ly/MrLansleyStrawmen

In terms of influencing the belief system of a policy-maker, this is nothing short of spectacular. The amount of professional lobbying that must have been involved in getting a busy Secretary of State to absorb and repeat these 12 strawmen must have been considerable.

Sadly, the evidence of the benefits failed to help make it into policy.[13] The evidence at that time was that, in the 10 years following the introduction of a 50p/unit minimum price in England, there would be:

- 960 fewer deaths
- 35,100 fewer hospital admissions
- £5.1bn in savings to the economy

The strawmen were more persuasive to the policy makers at that time, the drinks industry won, and people died as a result.

What has to change, and who has to change it?

> People need clean, clear information; it is as vital to health as clean, clear water

This, my final quotation in this chapter, is a short piece of great wisdom from the NHS Chief Knowledge Officer, Sir Muir Gray CBE.

As custodians or creators of evidence that could influence beneficial public policy, we have a responsibility to provide simplicity, clarity, certainty and security to the people who will turn evidence into policy.

We've learned that policy makers "ignore evidence that is difficult to interpret quickly", yet it is still common for creators of evidence to provide it in a way that is academic and aloof, complex, long and in a style that has been described as "decorated municipal gothic". Winston Churchill famously implored his War Cabinet to adopt brevity in their communications, and did it in a pithy, one-page memo[14].

We know that well-resourced lobbyists, paid to have regular contact with policy makers, have a variety of well-practised techniques to create doubt about our evidence in the minds of those policy makers.

---

[13] Results of Alcohol Strategy consultation: http://bit.ly/alcoholstrategyconsultation

[14] Winston Churchill on brevity in writing: http://bit.ly/WinstonBrevityMemo

My top 5 things that we need to do to overcome this are:

1. *Generate viscerality – get a strong sense of purpose for our evidence*

Viscerality is crucial to getting important things done. If your evidence is going to be important in getting vital public policy made, you need to recognise that there is a lot more to this than publishing or presenting a paper. You're going to need to adapt your strategy to counter the problems I've set out in this chapter, and this needs viscerality, a fire in the belly, more than it needs you to make any intellectual or style changes. Of course, if your evidence isn't important you won't need to do this.

2. *You need a plan*

It should be clear that a one-off presentation of your evidence isn't going to be enough to counter some of the obstacles I've described here. You need to plan how to gain power for your evidence from a very early stage. You'll need to identify advocates, mechanisms for how to drip feed your knowledge at the right times and in the right places.

3. *Research your policy makers*

WIIFM is an important thing to consider in any approach to a policy maker. It stands for 'what's in it for me?' and it is worth trying to find what makes them tick, whether they have any known prejudices and whether there could be any negative consequences to them in turning your evidence into policy.

4. *Become an expert in Agnotology[15] and the techniques of Denialism*

Remember that there may be people whose job is to sabotage the adoption of your evidence into policy. Learn the techniques they'll use and learn how to work against them. Become confident to publicly laugh at nonsense when the need arises.

5. *Deal with Regulatory Capture*

This can be potentially impossible to get past or work around. On an interpersonal level, it's embarrassing to admit that you've been cleverly

---

[15] The man who studies the spread of ignorance: http://bit.ly/agnotologyBBC

brainwashed, and you certainly won't gain influence by pointing this out to someone who you feel has been influenced by their involvement with industry representatives.

If a public sector organisation has taken the decision to work closely with business representatives, it's normally necessary to provide evidence to the top people that regulatory capture has occurred and is causing difficulty. Leadership and management action will be needed if the organisation is to reassert the necessary independent thought for it to properly represent the needs of stakeholders.

The USA has attempted to legislate against it, e.g. through the Regulatory Capture Prevention Act in 2011, but I don't expect that the UK will be ready for this for the foreseeable future.

If your evidence is important, follow the samurai code

Protect the weak; be equal to the strong; crush the wicked who would harm our people. Memorise it and turn it into one of your very own cognitive biases.

Public policy is far too important for good evidence to be ignored during its creation. People die, people suffer and society suffers a number of avoidable burdens.

Be a hero and do whatever it takes to get the public the policy they deserve.

~

Peter Wright has been an Environmental Health Officer for 35 years. He is convenor of the North East Public Health SkunkWorks, a loose alliance of people who want to look for new ways of "doing whatever it takes" to improve health and wellbeing in the region. Peter is known by the Chief Executive of his professional body as 'Mr Awkward', and by far less flattering names in other circles. Peter has been involved in a host of local, regional and national policy development work, and has found that decisions on policy are rarely based on what the evidence suggests is really needed.

Governments Should Create Our Money, Not Banks

Vincent Richardson and Alan Peyton
Supporters of Positive Money

In modern economies, it is a seldom understood fact that commercial banks create most of the money we use. The common misperception is that the state or central bank creates our money. We put the case here that this situation is far from the best way to create money because it helps create bubbles in property/stock markets which eventually burst, creating boom and bust cycles and ensuing subsequent problems for governments, the economy and society.

If instead, we allowed the state to create our money we would have a far more stable, transparent and democratic system.

The 2008 financial crash was a watershed moment in financial history and has led to much discussion as to how and why it happened and how we can stop it happening again.

We support and propose the ideas put forward by the Positive Money (PM) organisation.

Before 2007, 97% of the money we used in the UK existed in electronic form (similar to other countries) This money still exists as numbers representing total money 'balances' in national bank accounts. Only 3% of the money used was created by the state. This 3% is the notes and coins we use, which remains pretty much static over time, reflecting public demand for physical cash. So, the majority of the money we use today consists of electronic money in bank accounts.

The amount of money in existence varies with time. Banks actually create money through the process of making loans. Each time a bank loan is made, 'new money' is created and injected into the money supply. Money is also 'destroyed' in the same way when loans are repaid. When banks lend more than is repaid in loan repayments the amount of money in existence increases. Conversely, when bank lending falls below the rate of loan repayments then the amount of money in existence falls. This means that banks create about 97% of our money.

It is also important to note that this is not the only way money can be created. It is entirely possible for the state (via a central bank) to create all the money we need for our economy to work. We argue this would be entirely preferable because it would create a far more stable economy, less likely to suffer boom and bust cycles as well as reducing government spending crises, austerity and inequality.

What is the orthodoxy we are challenging?

The problem we face is that the current system is seen as the most effective way for money to be created and invested in modern economies. The orthodox assumption is that banks are best placed to ascertain how much money to create and where it is most effectively invested. Our heresy is to show that these assumptions are incorrect and that there is a valid workable alternative.

It is also assumed by many that governments have to borrow money from bond markets in order to balance budget deficits. We hope to show that this is also an incorrect assumption. Governments can in fact create money at will and have been doing so recently with Quantitative Easing (QE). However, the orthodox way of using QE means that money is simply spent into financial markets and does not reach or 'trickle down' to the real economy.

Who holds this orthodoxy?

This orthodoxy is held by numerous people and organisations:

The financial sector

The financial sector claims to understand the risks associated with creating money and lending it out. Banks have been doing this throughout their history. But they have a very bad record for 'over creating' money[1] which leads to periods of boom then bust, causing bank runs and collapse. This nearly always leads to wider economic malaise.

---

[1] Adair Turner claims that private banks left to their own devices will always 'over create' money.

Politicians

Generally, politicians do not understand banking and the money creation process[2] so banks tend to be left to their own malign operations.

Central banks (CBs)

Central banks have a primary objective to maintain 'financial stability'. This involves striving to keep the banks trading as far as possible in a crisis, even if this means allowing insolvent banks to continue trading. This is the so called 'moral hazard' dilemma, whereby CBs will rescue banks when normally they should allow them to fail. The main reason is that allowing banks to fail causes even more uncertainty in a panic and risks further bank failures. This means that banks are effectively immune from bad business decisions. Tim Geithner (former head of the New York Fed/US Treasury) admitted this was a necessary evil, even if it meant you end up "rewarding the arsonists who started the (2008) fire".

Regulators

Regulators have the task of ensuring that our banks are adequately regulated and supervised and say that, despite the massive failure of regulation and supervision prior to the 2007 crash, they now are putting into place 'better' regulation. They assure us this will prevent future serious bank failures. According to Positive Money and others, (like Martin Wolf, chief economic writer at the *Financial Times*) in reality little has changed other than very small increases in capital buffers. In the face of a panic like that of 2008, banks would again face slender capital buffers being wiped out, requiring further assistance by already hard-pressed central banks and taxpayers.

Most economists

Most economists have tended to ignore bank money creation as a potential problem, or even as a factor that that has more than a 'neutral' effect on the economy. Before 2007, very few economists spotted the coming crisis despite its enormous scale and resultant devastating consequences. Many

---

[2] A Positive Money poll of politicians found 85% of politicians do not understand how money is created in the modern economy.

have been moved to ask "how was it possible that none of them saw it coming?" including Her Majesty the Queen.

Most modern economic models used by economists do not factor money creation into their economic models. By and large, money creation by banks was considered to be a 'neutral' factor in the economy, something which now appears to be wide of the mark if not downright negligent.

University economics curriculums

Economic courses taught at universities fail to address or teach money creation by banks. Many students are now having to go to outside sources to find such information (such as Positive Money and the Rethinking Economics group).

What is our heresy?

Positive Money (PM) is an independent think tank set up after the 2008 financial crisis to discover what went wrong and to examine how we may put things right. The proposals put forward are based on an idea created by Irving Fisher and the Chicago School of Economics in the 1930s. This was in reaction to the bank-led crash of 1929 and ensuing economic depression. The lessons learnt from that historic crash can be just as easily applied to the financial global crisis that happened in 2008.

The major heretical proposal is that banks should not be allowed to create money at all. The second proposal, less controversial, is that the state be allowed to create our money instead (this is called Sovereign Money).

Money creation by banks is not well understood by the public or politicians. How do banks actually do this?

Banks create money when they make loans. This was recently been confirmed by The Bank of England when it said in its 2014 April Bulletin:

> In the modern economy, most money takes the form of bank deposits. But how those bank deposits are created is often misunderstood: the principal way is through commercial banks making loans.

> Whenever a bank makes a loan, it simultaneously creates a matching deposit in the borrower's bank account, thereby creating new money.

So what we have is a rather simple accounting trick that creates a 'liability' on one side of the bank balance sheet to match an 'asset' on the other. The asset is the actual loan agreement signed by the borrower and the matching liability is the creation of the borrower's money in the borrower's name in a bank account. At the moment the numbers are typed into the account, new money comes into existence.

Banks do not need to have access to other customers' savings or reserves to be able to carry out this procedure. What happens is the bank creates the liability (money) first and then worries about matching liabilities to assets later. It can do this by borrowing reserves from other banks on the inter-bank market or by encouraging depositors to deposit money with the bank.

Technically banks can increase their liabilities without legal limit and often do in a boom when credit is easy to obtain from other sources and demand for loans is high[3]. But it is just as easy for banks to get into liquidity problems when short-term funding dries up. Without that funding, banks are forced to sell off assets or raise more capital. Selling assets in an economic downturn causes asset prices to fall even further and a downward cycle amplifies. This is indeed what happened in the last financial crisis.

Approximately half of all bank assets (and hence lending) went into the property markets over the 10 years prior to the 2007 crisis (graph 1).

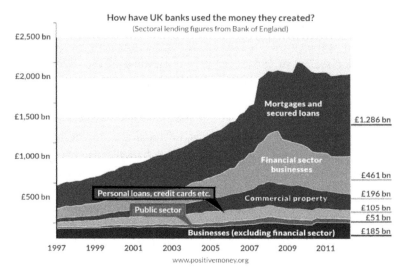

Graph 1: Where bank lending goes

---

[3] 'Where Does Money Come From; A guide to the UK monetary and banking system' (2011) Creative Commons.

Lending to the real wealth-generating part of the economy is very limited – in the period 1997-2007, UK businesses received less than 10% of all bank loans, so it is a myth that a primary function of banks is to help businesses with credit/loans. Banks on the whole do not like lending to small/medium size businesses as they are regarded as high risk with little collateral as security. For this reason businesses tend to rely on other sources of funding rather than the banks (e.g. credit cards, personal loans, family, friends, peer-to-peer lending or crowdfunding). In effect, UK banks have largely turned themselves into property and stock market lenders and are of little help to the real economy in obtaining credit. (In the same period, about 82% of all bank lending went into funding property and share purchases.)

From around the end of 2007, property price falls created huge problems for commercial banks due to the sheer volume of property assets on their books. Defaults increased, eroding bank profits and increasing enforced sales of repossessed properties. Bank profits fell and slender capital buffers went with them, causing insolvency.

Bank runs were also experienced for the first time in many years when Northern Rock faced queues of depositors wishing to remove their deposits. It took major intervention by the government of the day to avert a complete collapse of the bank. Eventually the biggest High Street bank, Royal Bank of Scotland (RBS) failed too. The "game was effectively up for British banking" (according to Chancellor Alistair Darling). He then had to implement a major bailout of the entire UK banking sector, nationalising almost half of the UK banks, seeing an end to the private running of the likes of RBS, HBOS and Lloyds in addition to many well-known historic Building Societies.

This collapse, when it came, was dramatic and echoed what happened in the USA, Ireland, Iceland, Spain, Cyprus, Portugal and decades earlier to Japan, South East Asia and Sweden. Major bank bailouts also happened in the Netherlands, Germany, France and Italy. The problem was very much a global one.

In the UK, prior to the crisis, UK banks created vast amounts of money via this system. The size of the money supply grew fourfold in 10 years. We can see from graph 2 the scale of the increase. This money was largely devoted to property lending (helping property prices into a bubble) with about a further 35% going into the financial markets (stock markets and company acquisitions). These two sectors accounted for around 85% of all bank lending.

UK property prices increased about three-fold during the same period.

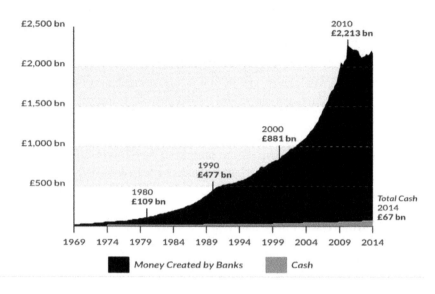

£2,500 bn

£2,000 bn

£1,500 bn

£1,000 bn

£500 bn

2010
£2,213 bn

2000
£881 bn

1990
£477 bn

1980
£109 bn

Total Cash
2014
£67 bn

1969   1974   1979   1984   1989   1994   1999   2004   2009   2014

■ Money Created by Banks   Cash

Graph 2, Money supply (Source: Bank of England)

Bank money creation is being directed toward assets that do not help the real wealth generating parts of our economy. UK bank lending increased existing asset prices (property markets and stock markets; with a rise of over 200% in the value of the FTSE 250 in the period 2009-2017). This only increased the asset wealth of those owning such assets, who are generally the wealthier sectors of the country. This increases inequality between the haves and have nots.

So we have a money creation system that enriches the already wealthy and is destined to cause boom and bust cycles that eventually collapse the banking sector that created it. This directly caused the ensuing recession and all the resulting problems that ran over into the wider economy and society: increased unemployment, government debt and austerity.

This is a damaging and self-defeating way to go about money creation.

Governments are also subsidising the banking sector by allowing banks to make profits and take high rewards in the good times only to have the public sector pay for their mistakes. Banks were unable to increase lending during the recession due to lack of general demand, making the money supply contract at exactly the time when more money was needed in the system. Banks have created too much when we did not need it and not enough when we needed more money in circulation. This is the system Positive Money wants to end.

PM first wants to end the banks' ability to create money. Under a PM system banks will still be able to lend, but they must have money before lending it. This would stop huge volumes of money being created out of thin air to cause property and stock market booms.

Second, PM would also create 100% safe deposit accounts as a by-product. The advantage of this would be that depositors' money could never disappear. In the event of a bank collapsing, a depositor's money would remain untouched. This avoids the need for governments to issue bank deposit insurance which is required under the current system to backstop bank liabilities (bank deposits), This would also help eliminate 'too-big-to-fail' banks. No bank would need to be bailed out should it become a victim of its own negligence. It could be safely allowed to fail.

Many critics claim that abolishing bank leverage in this way would stop credit creation and that money would become scarce as banks ration lending. The simple solution is for money creation to become a unique competence of the state.

The state is capable of creating more money in the same way that private banks do now. Recent government money creation in the form of QE has shown how this can be done. The Bank of England (BoE) can currently create money from nowhere by entering numbers into a computer and buying government debt (in the form of sovereign or government bonds) from financial institutions. In the same way, money could be handed over to the government to be 'spent' into the economy, rather than 'lent' into the economy by private banks.

The BoE also admits current QE is of limited, or no, use, going forward. As it current works, QE means that the BoE buys bonds from holders of those bonds (mainly financial institutions like pension funds, hedge funds, insurance companies and banks). So the new money created in this way has largely gone into the financial sector, which then uses that money mainly to buy property or more shares. This has had the effect of further increasing property prices and share/stock market prices. Very little of this new money has found its way down to the wider economy and so growth in the real economy has struggled to recover. Positive Money would like any future QE to happen as follows: the government should spend directly into the economy – thereby increasing public spending directly without having to borrow. This would help growth and not cause bubbles in property and stock markets. Positive Money (PM) calls this 'QE for the people'.

Studies by PM have shown that we need only take a fraction of the current QE (£445bn to date) to boost the economy where it matters. Returns on this 'QE for the people' would be £2.80 per £1 created, as opposed to the BoE estimate that the real economy gets a boost of just 8p for every £1 they have currently created.[4] Unfortunately, the BoE cannot do this at present.

By creating money in this way, the state can overcome recessions and shortages in the amount of money circulating in the economy.

Rather than just creating and lending new money, banks could lend on depositors' money only if they were open about where it was invested and provide specialist investment funds which would be at risk should the fund fail. There should be no state-backed guarantee for such funds. In this way, banks will become genuine 'intermediaries' – i.e taking money from depositors and lending it on to borrowers. This is what most people think banks do now, but as this chapter explains, this is not what banks do.

PM does not, however, propose to allow politicians access to the money-creation process. PM proposes that an independent technocratic committee be set up, similar to the current Monetary Policy Committee that sets interest rates. This committee of appointed experts would decide on the quantity of money creation required (monetary policy) to ensure a thriving economy (full employment). Once the decision has been made, money could be made available for the government of the day to spend. The politicians would then decide where to spend this money (fiscal policy) in a democratic and transparent way (according to political mandates). This method of money creation would ensure that there is a sensible separation of monetary and fiscal policy, also increasing democratic accountability to the money creation process.

Why are we right and the orthodoxy wrong?

Many senior public figures and economists have recently backed PM-style proposals: Mervyn King, Adair Turner (head of FSA during the last crisis), Martin Wolf (chief economic commentator at the *Financial Times*) and Ben Bernanke.

The IMF produced a paper[5] on the subject stating this idea would allow better control of business cycles, completely eliminate bank runs, reduce government debt and reduce levels of private debt.

Five Nobel-winning Economics Laureates have advocated the abolition of the system whereby banks create money via loans, meaning that only the

---

[4] BoE estimated £375bn of QE boosted the economy by 1.5-2% of GDP (£30bn).

[5] IMF Working Paper/12/202: 'The Chicago Plan Revisited'.

state should be allowed to do this, They are Milton Friedman, Merton Miller, James Tobin, George J. Stigler and Maurice Allais.

Estimates of the financial costs of the last crash vary from 10-15% of national GDP globally for every year since the crisis in affected developed nations.

Currently we have a system that requires individuals to take on ever more debt to get by and, without borrowers, there is no money in circulation. A Sovereign Money (SM) system would lower private debt levels as money would be created 'debt free'.

According to PM, banks receive approximately £25bn per year in subsidies simply by being allowed to create money, and that is a potential loss to the Exchequer each and every year.[6]

Regulation would also be made far easier. Current regulations are very complex, (e.g. the Basel Agreements and Dodd-Frank Act) often covering several thousands of pages. State-issued money would make regulation far simpler as the money would simply be issued as a payment by the government for goods/services or directly to our pockets as a 'citizens dividend'.

Alternative non-orthodox proposals

There are other organisations outside the orthodoxy (like PM) who have come up with different solutions to our money creation problems:

Digital/crypto currencies (like Bitcoin)

Whilst currencies like Bitcoin take some money-creation away from the banks it is not that useful to a national government wanting to control its own monetary/fiscal policy. A Sovereign Money system by contrast gives the government full scope to create/destroy money as and when required via spending and taxation.

These types of currencies can also encourage criminal activity as the money transactions are completely anonymous. Tax evasion, in particular, is seen as a threat and is being increasingly scrutinised by governments and its use restricted or even banned in some countries.

Such currencies are also prone to speculation and have become almost like a commodity in themselves. This detracts from the purpose of the

---

[6] http://bit.ly/kittens14

currency as 'good' money (a stable unit of exchange) since any 'good' money should (amongst other things) be stable in value.

Further disadvantages to digital currencies are that they are not widely accepted as payment and they are a comparatively slow.

That said, there is something to be said here about the blockchain technology behind digital currencies.

What is very exciting about blockchain is that it provides a potentially very good platform that may allow the central bank to issue its own 'digital' national currency. This would dramatically change the face of our money creation and payments system.

Such a national digital currency would in effect be Sovereign Money, which is what PM are proposing. This would enable the state to create and distribute newly created money quickly, with the added benefit that no-one anywhere has to go into debt.

The benefits would be: 100% safe bank deposits; eliminating bank runs; reducing the size of banks; a more stable financial sector.

If we succeed in creating such a blockchain-based digital national currency, we would have a Sovereign Money system evolve naturally. Encouragingly, central banks are now looking at and testing how this may become a reality.

Local Currencies; (like the Brixton pound/Swiss WIR currency)

These have proved popular and successful at a local level where money has become tight. However, under a wider SM system, there would be a better means of countering national money shortages through the state simply creating money to spend in the economy generally. This should eradicate (or greatly lessen) the need to have local currencies. Local currencies also do not address taxation issues as they normally have to be converted back to a national currency at some point.

Public Investment Banks

There are also proposals for national/local/public investment banks (as recently proposed by the Labour Party). PM sees no reason that such institutions could not run alongside a SM system if required, by creating money to fund local bank lending to aid regional economies. But, as with alternative/local currencies, they are not an answer to our problems in themselves.

Rather PM proposes the more comprehensive solution that money creation be left to the only truly democratically accountable body, the government.

Money creation is ultimately a 'sovereign power' and should not be allocated to any other body.

What has to change and who has to change it?

1. Take the power to create money away from the banks, or at least stop money creation for non-wealth generating sectors of the economy (property and stock markets).
2. Create money free of debt. This means the state 'spending' it into existence not banks 'lending' it into existence.
3. Spend newly created money into the productive part of the economy rather than financial markets and property bubbles.

We have to lobby our MPs and get them to understand this 'heresy' and demand a change in the current law.

~

Alan Peyton BSc and BA worked in HVAC industry until 1988. He switched to Business Analysis and Consultancy after an MBA in 1990 and Common Entrance qualification in Law 1991, involving extensive work in dealing with banks and finance until retirement in 2008. He insists that he was NOT to blame for the crash – the timing was merely coincidental!

Vincent Richardson BSc worked for Littlewoods retail stores, then a North East retail business until becoming self-employed. As a keen economics fan and business owner, he became fascinated by the financial crash of 2008 and its wider implications. He became a supporter of the Positive Money organisation in 2012 as a solution to the current problems of banking and money.

Driven to Distraction? A slow stroll to help local government re-connect with what matters

Catherine Hobbs

What is the orthodoxy that you are challenging?

When the performance management regime began in earnest in the late 1990s, it seemed to make good financial, value-for-money sense. It appeared to be a perfectly reasonable idea to measure the efficiency of investments being made in public service. At the outset, it would not have been reasonable to challenge this basic premise. Furthermore, it aimed to provide evidence of continuous improvement and thus sought to motivate a value-for-money culture of improvement, rather than what could be called a lazy, inefficient status quo. Fair enough. Again, this is a difficult thing to argue against. Performance management had a shaky start, but soon moved from less worthy descriptions of performance as 'outputs' (e.g. we have produced *x* reports) to more worthy descriptions of performance as 'outcomes' (e.g. we are making a difference to *x* people, or a facet of the environment – say air quality – is improving by *x*). Target setting soon became the norm for individuals, sections and departments to show that their inevitably fragmented funding streams were being well spent. Rather like the subtle build-up of tensions in an Alfred Hitchcock film, from innocence to guilt, a whole time-consuming, pressured culture of proof, measurement, explanations and competitiveness developed around it.

The Local Government Modernisation Agenda (LGMA) as a whole emerged from the Local Government White Papers of 1998 and 2001, introducing a range of policy initiatives. These initiatives were intended to lead to improvements which then would result in higher quality service, cost effectiveness, better responsiveness, more joined-up services, improved access for all groups, and increased user and staff satisfaction. Martin and

Bovaird (2005), in undertaking a meta-evaluation of the LGMA, concluded that more fundamental cross-boundary changes in service delivery would be needed, with bolder experimentation and innovation, expressing a viewpoint from case study authorities that the LGMA relied very heavily on funding, targets and inspection regimes dictated by central government. In particular, the latter viewpoint had not been conducive to local governance and local democracy, leading to a conclusion that a greater capacity for self-criticism and 'improving from within' would be needed.

Over the years, however, 'Performance Management' became a specialism in its own right, with complicated layers of target-setting at international, national, regional, sub-regional and local levels, rewards put in place incentivising the setting and achievement of 'stretch' targets, and the routine monitoring of achievement through 'milestones'. It became weirdly addictive and habit forming, even after the abolition of 4,700 central government targets by the coalition government in 2010 (Department for Communities and Local Government, 2010). Tracking measures nevertheless continued, with associated initiatives having already blossomed, such as benchmarking clubs and 'toolkit solutions' to help achieve quick wins. Such measures focused heavily on achieving cost savings within budget headings, rather than considering fundamentally new approaches to service provision and a variety of ways to define and judge success. Restricted rational management and planning techniques remained at the core of this activity, enabling the use of these performance management techniques as a tool to deliver what was required: for example, Labour authorities remained service-based in their approach and Conservative authorities progressed alternatives to in-house provision. The overall effect of this was to create a differentiated pattern of governance which reflected political and managerial intent more than a 'live' expression of serving local communities.

At the same time, professional service bodies became more likely to strengthen their position within this regime by linking it to training and performance. Yet, taking pause, community-focused approaches in local government should surely not be about professional, market or managerial models, nor even solely an individual user-focus, but should also relate to collective interests and the debating of the common good as circumstances evolve. Thus, the intended breadth of review to develop fundamental improvements actually staggered in a quagmire of minutiae of measurement.

The assumption that performance can be measured in order to compare the performance of local authorities using sets of indicators had already been questioned (Boyne, 1997), and a suggestion had been made that a more strategic approach was required rather than being purely about service provision, with associated efforts needed in building the skills and technologies to secure proper reform (Martin, 1999). Furthermore, a serious danger was identified that, amidst all of this, the client can remain a minor player in the organisational change process (Lawton et al., 2000).

Moving on to Comprehensive Performance Assessment (CPA), an overview of CPA in local government (Game, 2006) found that, even though 51% of councils were rated as excellent or good, headlines focused on the minority who had been assessed as poor or weak, resulting in disputes, injunctions, court cases and complaints about flawed methodology which failed to recognise external constraints for particular authorities, such as areas of economic deprivation. A growing reliance in public service on the measurement of performance and results had also led to unintended consequences, including forms of 'gaming'. For example, a bus driver who is incentivised to run the service to time fails to stop at all bus stops (Greiling, 2006) and patients are made to wait outside hospitals in ambulances until they could be seen within the four-hour limit (Bevan & Hood, 2006). Guilfoyle (2012) also picks up on the preponderance (and inevitability) of gaming, identifying its relevance to the arena of policing, concluding that research is needed to close the gap between theory and practice, particularly from an ethnographic and systems perspective, in order to enrich the understanding of systemic interdependencies.

A 30-year review considered what has been learned through a 'governance by numbers' approach (Jackson, 2011). Jackson highlighted the naive goal model, pointing out that public sector performance is multi-dimensional; allocative efficiency had suffered neglect, and also other important considerations were absent (equity, environmental impact, ethics). At the same time, consultants' and trainers' literature remained prescriptive and, with limits to 'the linear path', there is a lack of a general theory of public sector performance. This brings us up to a point where a reward system has been built around the production of data, rather than effectiveness in serving clients' needs. So how, after all these years, do we move beyond the Outcomes-based Performance Management approach (Lowe & Wilson, 2017)?

I am thus joining others in challenging this orthodoxy of the performance management culture. I argue that apparently reasonable moves towards performance management have, over the years, created an unreasonable distraction. Unintended consequences have been pointed out by reasonable critics who tend to be branded as dissenters, thus engendering a blinkered view of the meaning of, and potential for, improvement, preventing a joined-up approach towards a more authentic public service effectiveness linked with purpose, values and adaptability at the local level. The performance management culture, born of a reasonable sense of accountability, has trapped us into accepting certain ways of thinking and accounting for ourselves. The performance management culture needs itself to self-improve. As an orthodoxy, it has crept in sideways and often remains unquestioned.

Where is it held?

In my experience, although its heyday could be said to have abated, this approach has persisted over the decades (with inevitable variations) in local government. As partially hinted above, this goes much wider – including central government, health agencies and the police. In other words, this orthodoxy is held within the public policy design system in general.

Who holds it?

This 'orthodox' view is held by all promoters of an efficiency agenda which is not considered within a wider context, particularly those who are wedded to a form of accountability relating only to the variations in pre-determined financial budget headings. Perhaps it began as a 'value for money' assumption – i.e. a way of accountability for effective spending. It is rife, because it is a difficult thing to argue against. The idea of a triple bottom line (financial, social, environmental) (Elkington, 1998) has not been popular in UK government, as financial accountability has been allowed to predominate. Valiant attempts are being made to inject more sense into performance management through the Public Sector Scorecard (PSS) but organisations and departments with established performance frameworks have been reluctant to do any more than minor updates (Moullin, 2017). More optimistically, there are glimmers of a common light developing at the end of the many tunnels: a review of ambulance service targets has finally asked 'what counts?' rather than 'what can be counted?' (Moullin, 2018). At the same time, although there are considerable challenges for the UK's combined authorities in achieving success, they aim to move towards pooled funding, joined-up thinking, local leadership and multi-agency responsibility (Murphie, 2018). These could be hopeful signs that the orthodoxy of performance management is at least moving towards a more sophisticated level of maturity.

What is your heresy?

The performance management regime has created significant time-hungry demands for professionalism, de-personalised the workplace and in effect has suggested a fake linear cause-effect concept of efficiency. This approach has had unintended consequences which, collectively, have driven a talented professional resource to distraction. For example, an environmental policy professional who spends more time interpreting targets and milestones, has less time to devise and enact policy improvements. It's been expensive to implement, while favouring short-termism and an over-emphasis on impact rather than a more fundamental questioning of social purpose. It has also favoured a 'fast pace', reinforced silos and failed to consider collective achievement more intelligently.

A focus on performance management has resulted in the shrinking of the subtler and richer skills of human endeavour within public policy – where thinking can be dismissed as a waste of time. Yet not taking the time to think properly, both individually and together, is surely the biggest waste of time of all. This occurs daily in specialist fields, right up to a meta level; consider Stern's sage observation that, by looking at the environment through the lens of the economy, "climate change presents a unique challenge for economics: it is the greatest and widest-ranging market failure ever seen." (Stern, 2006, pg. i). There has been a lack of genuine collaboration, reflexivity, connectedness with what really matters. It's been eyes down, rather than heads up.

So, in order to begin to be constructive, what has been missing? The performance management regime itself, although it had reasonable beginnings, did not sufficiently question its *own* performance through time, its effect on working patterns and structures, its own use of resource, or what might be missing (or harmful) about assessing individuals, sections or departments of public service organisations as a form of fractured, silo-based assessment of public service efficiency. Targets became a mixture of measures relating (of course) to what *can* be measured, to a myriad of measures linked with 'customer service' as well as outcome (e.g. answering the phone within x rings – might feedback about a sense of being listened to have been better?). Targets and measurement snowballed out of control, but retained their credibility as something that it was desirable to spend time on. To this day, it remains difficult to question this approach without appearing to be an obstructive dissenter, rather than a well-meaning critic whose heart is in the right place. Who can argue with a desire to prove that a measurable difference has been made, that focusing on 'proof' of 'what works' where possible is important in public service? Again, proof of what works, works only up to a point (and a proper argument about 'what works' in local government would be a whole new chapter). It is part of the bigger story. We've actually been missing the *human* endeavour, but we can recover it. Instead of quickly trying to prove results, we need to be willing to slow down and move our attention elsewhere.

Why are you right, and why is the orthodoxy wrong?

To answer this question we need to delve into the realm of uncertainty and paradox.

I believe I am right to question. I think it's useful to retain the better aspects of the evaluation process and ensure that an established routine of performance management can accept the subtler, qualitative aspects of effective public policy making. It could be so much more discerning and intelligent. The risk is that we are measuring the detail and missing the bigger picture, or measuring the big picture, and missing the important detail, focused instead upon turning our good people, including our bright young people and our experienced older people, into hollowed-out technocrats. There are, perhaps, better ways to navigate these risks in order to become more resilient (e.g. Bovaird & Quirk, 2013). The results of lifetimes of wider thought over the generations are there for the learning, but these are being consistently 'othered' by the sheer tenacity and lazy simplicity of the accepted ways. We need to own up and wise up to this.

It is sometimes better to admit to being wrong or uncertain and learn from that, rather than continuing a simplistic pretence of always knowing and being right. Retaining the *pretence* of being right (though sometimes, admittedly, a necessary tactic) in *all* circumstances is what is wrong. Spending time to realise you are uncertain about something can sometimes be beneficial, yielding positive influences that could not have been predicted.

So, I am right to be wrong, to question, be uncertain, make mistakes (and learn from that) and the orthodoxy is wrong to claim to be right, or fail to admit when mistakes have been made (all the time).

What has to change, and who has to change it?

First, we must slow down. We can't measure everything that matters. The insatiable demand for measurement creates a sense of urgency and distraction which renders us incapable of a broader form of perception which is possible if we slow down. This slowing down could take many forms, but here are a few suggestions.

Slowing down – a habit of questioning

Instead of going along with 'fast-pace' and a focus on doing, it may be better to get into the habit of slowing down and asking: is this the appropriate thing to do in these circumstances? What will the cost of the exercise be and is it telling us what we really need to know? What's missing from our calculations? Are we asking good enough questions? Could the aim of a research project be to generate better questions as a form of result?

Slowing down – what is good information?

Amidst the growing ability of technology to handle large amounts of data, there is a danger that the data are not rigorous enough. People love data and charts and are not prone to question the validity of the data itself once displayed visually in a smart format. The role of data scepticism and data curation becomes increasingly important, taking on board the view of Bateson (1979, p.212) that information is "any difference that makes a difference". There is a difference between a piece of information defined as something we can measure, and something that makes a difference. There is one world but, inevitably, multiple versions of it, where understanding this variety is the key to unlocking a more complex, creative and dynamic form of sense-making through a process of data curation.

Slowing down – longer-term view of effectiveness

Rather than a short-term view of efficiency and 'proving' results to a short timescale, slowing down permits a longer-term view of flexibility for effectiveness. We often perhaps hear or read 'no magic formula' or 'no silver bullet' – that remains the case, so why do we persist in peering into this falsely simplified dark abyss of quick-fix 'solutions'? It's a Plato's cave experience, where we have come to believe that the mere shadows we have created in a cave are the real world: if some refer to the possibility of a more complex reality in order to be more effective, they fear being ridiculed or –

even worse – risk losing their livelihood if they divert from the mainstream view of shadows.

Slowing down – adaptive learning pathway for systemic leadership

I have proposed a different approach with a core focus on collaborative learning, working differently together. Through the experience of my doctoral research I developed, as an example, an Adaptive Learning Pathway for Systemic Leadership (Hobbs, 2019). It draws upon a range of established approaches including complexity, systems thinking and operational research in order to cultivate capacity-building in social learning. It is structured around a five-stage sequence of questioning (Why adapt? Who and why? Wider context? What? How?), each of which goes back to the basis of what matters (thinking differently matters, assumptions matter, wider contexts matter, people matter and systemic effectiveness matters). For each of the five learning points, there is an operational principle (collaborative learning, critical appraisal, dynamic diagnostic, participation and clarity of purpose), each of which signposts useful resources for dealing with this facet of a systemic issue. This is thus about social learning to re-connect with purpose in order to be more effective, rather than to measure 'results' quickly based on goals or targets. As there are sixteen resources in all, substantial education/training and a style of co-research between academia and practitioners is needed in order to avoid the superficiality of an applied 'toolkit' approach. This approach is not prescriptive, it's about building human capability to deal with the complexity of real-world issues. There's quite a long way to go.

You challenge...

The stepping stone to a different approach, like many other transitions, is likely to be a widespread movement of small-scale willingness-to-challenge, rather than a sudden acceptance by the powers-that-be. In order to do the right thing, we have to consciously question and stop doing the wrong thing, or letting the wrong thing happen. This is especially difficult if you believe your reputation or livelihood depends on it – but, does it? Although the performance management element of New Public Management could be said to have already evolved towards some form of New Public Governance or Network Governance, each phase of change has left its mark and continues in some way; local authorities have responded variously from their differing circumstances, leaving a fragmented landscape in which the present continues to rub shoulders with the past. Individuals thus need to challenge within the highly tailored context of what makes sense locally. So, when we get to the question of *who* has to change the orthodoxy of performance management, there is cause for great optimism, as this is happening already as a form of social movement. A widescale retrenchment of responsibility was never going to be created by austerity-driven measures, resulting in a shrunken role for local government. If anything, the opposite has happened: the stewardship role of a democratically elected local government is as important as ever. This gets to the core purpose of local government: not (only) to act as a service provider and commissioner, but to take on a role of stewardship for decision-making within the local area about what matters in relation to local people, the economy and the environment. Local government practitioners need to be able to occupy their time as local public servants, not as one-trick ponies created by a bygone age of a centrally-created performance regime.

Who? – cause for optimism

There has already been a magnificent degree of self-organising to address the wide-ranging challenges presented by the local government reform agenda, with substantial academic attention also being paid to the concept of public value, based on a strategic triangle of the authorising environment, operational capacity and public value outcomes (Moore, 1995; Benington, 2009; Benington & Moore, 2010). Many transitional ideas have been cultivated through initiatives such as the Commission on 2020 Public Services (2010) which proposed, amongst other things, a shift in culture from social security to social productivity and the Leeds Commission on the Future of Local Government (2012) which promoted a spirit of civic enterprise and the exploration of finding new ways of working between the public, private and third sectors.

We can consider two causes for optimism:

Cause for optimism (1) – micro-level from the ground up

There has been a blurring of the boundaries between the roles of the public, private and third sectors, and worthy initiatives have encouraged a more place-based, joined-up approach largely led by amendments to funding streams, such as Total Place and Whole Place Community Budgets, Creative Councils, Cooperative Councils Innovation Network and the Public Service Transformation Network.

There is much cause for optimism, for much striving is present in turning attention to finding more effective ways to address complexity, from the mainstream of practice, from research and from the grey literature of commentary. To name but a few, and in no particular order, the Integration and Implementation Science initiative (Bammer, 2013), Relating Systems Thinking and Design (Ryan, 2014; Veale, 2014), the People's Powerhouse initiative (IPPR North & Transform Lives Company, 2017), the RSA Action and Research Centre (Conway et al., 2017), the OECD (Observatory of Public Sector Innovation, 2017), the Lankelly Chase Foundation (Abercrombie et al., 2015), the experimental work of various Policy Labs in the UK and abroad, and the crucial issue of funding arrangements for complexity (Knight et al., 2017). It was pointed out some time ago that fashionable business ideas create their own demand: a more robust and sustainable form of capacity-building for core competencies in dealing with wicked issues more effectively is the proper order of the day (Hood & Lodge, 2004). It has been well argued that a collaborative public service should be as much about alchemy as science, and the capacity for collaboration needs helping, rather than hindering by an out-dated form of business case, target-based measurement and tools for returns on investment (Wilson et al., 2016).

Are we there yet?

It seems to be a mixed bag at present. Some people are still moving fast to repeat the same efforts (and mistakes), while others are more willing to slow down to achieve something more substantial longer-term. So, if certain ways of working by measurement are still entrenched in some quarters of mainstream local government, how can emphasis be given to the capacity-building required in the area of systems thinking?

Perhaps half way?

When Jake Chapman (2004) produced his first edition of *System Failure: Why governments must learn to think differently*, he suggested that, if a new generation has to grow up with a new way of thinking in order for it to find acceptance, rather than existing adults 'seeing the light', then a 30-year cycle for a generation of civil servants and politicians to die off would be far from ideal, as would the tactic of waiting for a catastrophic failure of public policy before systems ideas were taken up. Perhaps time is on our side, as we are already half way there, but it would be good if there could be a general impetus towards building the practical capacity in a variety of systems thinking approaches over the next fifteen years to slow down the current ways of working, but speed up our effectiveness. There is some catching up to do in capacity building, styles of leadership and craftsmanship, the job market and research funding mechanisms.

Cause for optimism (2) – macro commentary about social movement of revival

Dunn's social learning

Although widespread micro-level activity can ultimately have a macro effect, none of the above ground-up optimism implies any significant abatement to the ingrained habit of measurement of performance, evaluation and so on. It is natural that this should continue, but only up to a point. The distraction that has been (and could be) created by this must be reflected upon and weighed up against better ways of using the resource of time and also human resource. Consideration should be given to a more flexible culture, where professionals are able to use the skills appropriate for a particular context. Rhodes (2016) describes this as recovering the craft of public administration. Also, the characteristics of the 21st-century public servant identified by Needham and Mangan (2014) incorporate a wide range of roles, including distributed and collaborative models of leading, reflection on practice and learning from that of others. In order to achieve Dunn's fourth human threshold within human-social evolution of 'social learning' (Dunn, 1971)[1], in which we can escape deterministic models of economics and the social sciences, we have to be willing to think, and think together – accepting a social learning metaphor which is open and creative, rather than programmed. Dunn identified such social learning as being able to commit to both science and human values, and saw Systems Theory as a significant portal to this social learning metaphor.

Conclusion: hamster wheel or a better way?

> *It's about culture; we're on a hamster wheel and thinking is perceived as a waste of time.*
> Local government representative (Hobbs, 2016)

---

[1] Threshold 1: Symbolization (speech and communication); Threshold 2: Social maintenance (social systems and groups); Threshold 3: Classical scientific method (industrial and technological revolution); Threshold 4: Social learning.

Lack of thinking time is often blamed, yet each of us *is* responsible – we can't continue to pretend we're helpless, so busy within our self-created hamster wheels.

A better way: the role of research as how to succeed in reality

The role of research is crucial. We have to overcome the dysfunctional market between local government research and practice (Allen et al., 2014). As Lazenby wrote in 2015, taking up the viewpoint of local government managers – "plane crash survivors do not need telling 'look what I've discovered: you're in the desert and you need water!'" From scholarly work, they need "solid, research-based tools we can use to succeed in this reality" (Lazenby, 2015, p. 62). This approach is surely best developed as a combined effort of co-research, to make the research both scholarly and relevant to practice (Pettigrew, 1997). Whether in research or practice, it's difficult to move away from the cultural domination of instrumentalism: this is not a linear argument, but a synergistic gathering drawn from the wonderful 'mess' of practice. It has also been pointed out that co-creation without systems thinking can be dangerous (Midgley, 2016), giving emphasis to the crucial importance of building capacity and knowledge of a *range* of systems thinking practices.

Discussions about data *per se* can absorb inordinate amounts of time and resource: this can, without checking, become spurious proof of some sort of pseudo-science which often fails to take into account the all-important human and behavioural issues (by which, as a psychologist, I mean understanding and respecting human behaviour, not purely with regard to manipulating it). Continuing a restrictive and domineering discussion about measurement of results is a partial approach which remains painfully inadequate. Up to a point, measurement makes good sense, if performed intelligently. This chapter is not anti-measurement. But a tide of data is upon us, and continuing demands for measurement at all costs could be creating a virtual straitjacket for us all. A better way would see the necessary accountability taking on a sensible level of performance measurement *and* ongoing learning through dialogue as supplementary to each other (Lewis & Triantafillou, 2012). Could the role of research be rooted in this better way?

A better way: a range of viewpoints

How you perceive this chapter will depend on your own initial viewpoint. Given that you are reading this book in the first place, you will hopefully not find it too heretical. You may see it as uncomfortable; you may well, hopefully and healthily, contest certain points, or you may even be heaving a sigh of relief that at last someone has expressed these somewhat imperfect thoughts. It is this *range* of viewpoints that is the most valuable thing of all: they should not be repressed as we all fall into a tacit acceptance. By doing so, we are doing the skills and professionalism of humanity a great disservice. The social learning to be had by questioning, discussing and debating these issues will be way beyond measurement: incalculable and invaluable.

I am currently engaged in exploring the potential for Critical Systems Thinking (Jackson, 2019) to help build the capacity to address complexity in the public sector. This approach demands a slowing down from the 'fast-pace,' finding ways of creating space for deliberation and, following the fall-out from the performance management regime, re-connecting with what matters: thinking differently, assumptions, wider contexts, people and systemic effectiveness. This moves towards the arena of public purpose, taking into account contemporary needs and constraints adaptively in a way which can be tailored to the locality.

My conclusion, which is distilled, rather than deduced (Weick, 1979, p. 40), is this: by denying people – whether employees or the wider community – an opportunity for authentic deliberation about something more valuable than numbers or finance, we are normalising a process of social failure.

> The subjective is not derived from some one person's observations and thoughts; it rather derives from a social agreement not to examine the foundations of beliefs beyond a certain point. (Churchman, 1970, p. B-48)

~

Catherine Hobbs hails from the north west of England and has analysed much data, conducted at-the-scene accident investigations and a national attitude survey, developed and monitored multi-agency road safety strategies and integrated local transport plans in academic, national park and local government settings. With a BSc (Hons) in psychology (Aston) and an MSc Local Governance (Institute for Local Government Studies, University of Birmingham) Catherine, driven by her fascination with the need for capacity-building in public sector reform, has recently completed her doctoral research at the Centre for Systems Studies (University of Hull) about learning for systemic leadership within local governance networks.

References

Abercrombie, R., Harries, E., & Wharton, R. (2015) *Systems Change: a Guide to what it is and how to do it*, New Philanthropy Capital

Allen, T., Grace, C., & Martin, S. (2014) *From Analysis to Action: Connecting Research and Local Government in an Age of Austerity*. Report of the Local Government Knowledge Navigator, Institute for Government

Bammer, G. (2013) *Disciplining Interdisciplinarity: Integration and Implementation Sciences for Researching Complex Real-World Problems*, Australian National University E Press

Bateson, G. (1979) *Mind and Nature: A Necessary Unity*, Hampton Press

Benington, J. (2009) 'Creating the public in order to create public value?' *International Journal of Public Administration, 32*(3-4), 232-249

Benington, J., & Moore, M. H. (2010) *Public Value: Theory and Practice*, Palgrave Macmillan

Bevan, G., & Hood, C. (2006) 'What's measured is what matters: targets and gaming in the English public health care system', *Public Administration, 84*(3), 517-538

Bovaird, T., & Quirk, B. (2013) Risk and Resilence. In C. Staite (Ed.), *Making sense of the future: can we develop a new model for public services?* Institute of Local Government Studies, University of Birmingham

Boyne, G. (1997) 'Comparing the performance of local authorities: An evaluation of the audit commission indicators', *Local Government Studies, 23*(4), 17-43

Chapman, J. (2004) *System Failure: Why Governments Must Learn to Think Differently*, 2nd ed, Demos

Churchman, C. W. (1970) 'Operations research as a profession', *Management Science, 17*(2), B-37-B-53

Commission on 2020 Public Services (2010) 'From Social Security to Social Productivity', 2020 Public Services Trust at the RSA

Commission on the Future of Local Government (2012) Final Report.

Conway, R., Masters, J., & Thorold, J. (2017) *From Design Thinking to Systems Change: how to invest in innovation for social impact*. The Royal Society of Arts

Department for Communities and Local Government (2010) 'Councils' red tape cut as 4,700 Whitehall targets slashed', Retrieved 6 December 2017, from http://bit.ly/kittens07

Dunn, E. S. (1971) *Economic and Social Development: A Process of Social Learning*, The Johns Hopkins Press

Elkington, J. (1998) 'Partnerships from cannibals with forks: The triple bottom line of 21st-century business', *Environmental Quality Management, 8*(1), 37-51

Game, C. (2006) 'Comprehensive performance assessment in English local government', *Int. Journal of Productivity and Performance Management, 55*(6), 466-479

Greiling, D. (2006) 'Performance measurement: a remedy for increasing the efficiency of public services?' *Int. Journal of Productivity and Performance Management, 55*(6), 448-465

Guilfoyle, S. (2012) 'On target?—Public sector performance management: recurrent themes, consequences and questions', *Policing, 6*(3), 250-260

Hobbs, C. (2016) 'Tapping the resource within? Exploring a learning pathway for systemic leadership within local governance networks' (unpublished doctoral dissertation), University of Hull

Hobbs, C. (2019) *Systemic Leadership for Local Governance: tapping the resource within,* Palgrave Macmillan

Hood, C., & Lodge, M. (2004) 'Competency, bureaucracy, and Public Management reform: A comparative analysis', *Governance, 17*(3), 313-333

IPPR North, & Transform Lives Company (2017) *The People's Powerhouse: Putting the People in the Northern Powerhouse,* IPPR

Jackson, M. C., (2019) *Critical Systems Thinking and the Management of Complexity: Responsible Leadership for a Complex World,* Wiley

Jackson, P. M. (2011) 'Governance by numbers: what have we learned over the past 30 years?' *Public Money & Management, 31*(1), 13-26

Knight, A. D., Lowe, T., Brossard, M., & Wilson, J. (2017) *A Whole New World: Funding and Commissioning in Complexity,* Collaborate

Lawton, A., McKevitt, D., & Millar, M. (2000) 'Developments: Coping with Ambiguity: Reconciling External Legitimacy and Organizational Implementation in Performance Measurement', *Public Money & Management, 20*(3), 13-20

Lazenby, S. (2015) 'Commentary: The roles of local government managers: a view from the trenches', *Public Administration Review, 75*(1), 62

Lewis, J. M., & Triantafillou, P. (2012) 'From performance measurement to learning: a new source of government overload?' *International Review of Administrative Sciences, 78*(4), 597-614

Lowe, T., & Wilson, R. (2017) 'Playing the game of outcomes-based performance management. Is gamesmanship inevitable? Evidence from theory and practice', *Social Policy & Administration, 51*(7), 981-1001

Martin, S. (1999) 'Developments: Visions of Best Value: Modernizing or just muddling through?' *Public Money & Management, 19*(4), 57-61

Martin, S., & Bovaird, T. (2005) 'Service improvement: A progress summary from the meta-evaluation of the Local Government Modernisation Agenda', ODPM

Midgley, G. (2016) Co-creation without systems thinking can be dangerous. Retrieved from http://bit.ly/kittens10

Moore, M. H. (1995) *Creating Public Value: Strategic Management in Government*, Harvard University Press

Moullin, M. (2017) 'Improving and evaluating performance with the Public Sector Scorecard', *Int. Journal of Productivity and Performance Management, 66*(4), 442-458

Moullin, M. (2018) Flawed targets and the ambulance service – is there a happy ending? Retrieved 15 January 2018, from http://bit.ly/kittens08

Murphie, A. (2018) *Growth through devolution: A New Year's outlook*. Retrieved from http://bit.ly/kittens11

Needham, C., & Mangan, C. (2014) *The 21st Century Public Servant*, University of Birmingham

Observatory of Public Sector Innovation (2017) *Working with Change: Systems Approaches to Public Sector Challenges*, OECD

Pettigrew, A. M. (1997) 'The Double Hurdles for Management Research' in T. Clarke (Ed.), *Advancement in Organizational Behaviour: Essays in Honour of D.S. Pugh* (pp. 277-296), Dartmouth Press

Rhodes, R. A. W. (2016) 'Recovering the Craft of Public Administration', *Public Administration Review, 76*(4), 638-647

Ryan, A. J. (2014) 'A framework for systemic design', *Formakademisk, 7* (4, Art. 4), 1-14

Stern, N. (2006) *Stern Review Report on the Economics of Climate Change*, Executive Summary, HM Treasury

Veale, J. A. (2014) 'Systemic Government and the Civil Servant: a new pattern for systemic design', *Formakademisk, 7* (3, Art. 1), 1-25

Weick, K. E. (1979) *The Social Psychology of Organizing: Second Edition*, Addison-Wesley

Wilson, R., Jackson, P., & Ferguson, M. (2016) Editorial: 'Science or alchemy in collaborative public service? Challenges and future directions for the management and organization of joined-up government', *Public Money & Management, 36*(1), 1-4

Managers Nearly Always Measure the Wrong Things

Richard Davis
Vanguard Consulting

What is the orthodoxy that you are challenging?

In my 30 years I have yet to come across an organisation that had measures that told it how well it met purpose.

I have worked in many planning departments. They had measures of how long it took them make a decision on an application. On the face of it this might seem to be helpful to applicants but, in reality, what the applicant needs is for the planners to say 'yes' to an application that solves the applicant's problem and is acceptable or good for the local environment. All the measures achieved was to convert a 2% refusal rate into a 30% refusal rate because it was easier to determine an application in the time frame by refusing it.

Where is it held?

The health system is replete with dubious measures. The four-hour A&E target may be helpful to a few but is largely irrelevant and simply causes people to be admitted when they don't need to be or to be stuck in ambulances waiting to get in. Treatment targets and health screening have resulted in people being over-diagnosed and subjected to unnecessary procedures. Screening is utterly plausible and sometimes the right thing to do. Equally it often the wrong thing to do. Turning people into patients is not a good system.

The banks and other finance organisations measure market share. How does that help the customer? What it has done is to turn branches into sales centres and demoted the manager to an administrator who has not the authority nor the wherewithal to solve the customer's problems and that's if you are lucky enough to find a branch or get an appointment with the manager. We have 'relationship managers' who in reality only serve to help the customer solve problems that should never have arisen in the first place if the bank systems worked.

Many organisations have customer satisfaction measures and it is tempting to think that this will help them understand how well they meet purpose. But the fact that most of these measures result in 85-95% outcomes tells you nothing. Unless the organisation has done anything exceptionally good or bad, customers respond with an anodyne, 'it's all right really'. Measurement of customer satisfaction hides a bigger sin though. I was working with a South African bank in a department that served small businesses. They had an enviably high satisfaction rating. We sent their staff out to ask customers what mattered to them in terms of how they wanted to run their business and how the bank could help them with what mattered. Once they were asked how well the bank delivered against what mattered, every single customer said, "they don't".

What has to change?

My starting point is always to determine the purpose of the organisation – from the customer's perspective. If I am that customer or (if it is a public sector organisation) the citizen – we should never call citizens customers – then what problem of mine is that organisation claiming to solve? This leads to the next vital question: if they know their purpose, is the organisation measuring how well they achieve it? It remains a truism that you get what you count. If you don't measure it, you don't get it. Deming's advice to job applicants was that they should tell their prospective employer, 'tell me what you measure and I'll tell you what I can do for you'.

Purpose can be an illuminating conversation. Vanguard has worked with many social housing organisations. What is the purpose of social housing? A view I would support is that it should be, wherever possible and appropriate, to help people get *out* of social housing. In other words, we could be helping people develop the capability to grow and thrive and therefore move on. However, the original social housing promoted tenancy for life. Much housing stock has been passed on to housing associations and their *de facto* purpose is to get and keep good tenants.

The consequence then of failing to measure purpose is not only that it is not delivered but the original purpose of the organisation becomes distorted or even lost altogether.

Why is this? Is it really that difficult to measure purpose? Well no, not at all. It is just as easy to measure the right things as it is to measure the wrong things. We have helped many organisations do it and they find it liberating. Customers love it, unsurprisingly, and staff love being purposeful – it is what they joined the organisation for in the first place. It also leads to efficiencies, cost savings and productivity improvement.

I know a team in South Wales who care for people with dementia. The manager decided that they were worrying too much about what the commissioners wanted and not enough about what mattered to the people they were charged to look after, let alone what mattered to those people's families. He told his team to do what mattered in whatever way their (extensive) knowledge and experience told them. Your purpose, he said, as if he needed to, is to help people live a good life and die a good death.

He defined *his* role as keeping the system off the team members' backs. The results have been astonishing. None of the people being cared for has had to leave their home and go into residential care. Local GPs have been heard to comment that they thought Mr/Mrs So and So was dead as they hadn't seen them for months. Staff morale and satisfaction is at an all-time high – staff are enjoying their role again. And what happened to cost? It went down and capacity went up. The manager had to agree with the commissioner to fudge the definitions so that they could use, not lose, the capacity that they had created. The staff had reconnected people with friends, neighbours, family, old work colleagues and local charities such that their attention was 'little and often' rather than intensive. Some of the most effusive complements came from the families – the team had helped them every bit as much during a very worrying and distressing time. If you ask the manager if it has been difficult, he would say only initially. The main thing had been the courage to do what was right in spite of the system.

I have struggled to find an adequate reason for the near universal failure to measure the right things and be true to purpose. I know how punishing the current target systems are both in the public and private sectors. I know, also, how punishing the regulation system is – not only do you get what you count, but you get what the regulator pays attention to. Just think of the times as a customer you are security checked when you contact many organisations and yet very few of those transactions require it. The interpretation of the pressure from regulation has caused these organisations to set up their IT so that the operator cannot get into their system until they have security checked the customer. They cannot tell you the time of day until they have security checked you.

A consequence is that people with the courage to design their service to meet purpose are often made pariahs because they expose their seniors to accusations of failing to meet targets and regulation.

One of our clients in social housing achieved stunning results. Tenant satisfaction (about what really mattered) soared, rent arrears dropped and evictions plummeted. 95% of repairs were carried out *before* the appointment date. And yet the regulator marked them down for not meeting appointments – it is that stupid. That manager is no longer employed and has moved on.

Similarly, a neurology consultant re-designed the pathway for stroke patients against what he could see mattered most for each patient. He saved lives, improved outcomes for many (which meant significantly better quality of life) and saved huge amounts of money by not having to carry out expensive procedures either then or later. Unfortunately for him and his patients the hospital was put in the position of losing money as they were paid a tariff per procedure. That consultant no longer works at that hospital.

The regulatory system can be brutal. I worked with an 'intentional' community. They operated as a group of volunteer families who take in people with learning difficulties and helped them live mutually beneficial lives operating smallholdings and craft activities. The trustees became overly concerned about failing regulation inspections and brought in ex-care home managers to run it. The community essentially no longer exists, having been converted into something that violates its original values and principles. The trustees thought they were doing the right thing and were not bad people – they simply felt they had no choice.

Much of this comes from government, but government only reflects what we have taught managers. Ministers like to talk about 'evidence-based policy' but this is clearly a fig leaf. They are, and never have been, interested in evidence either to design policy or to evaluate it. Policy is designed by needing to have 'big ideas' and, once agreed, the civil service has the job of implementing it regardless. The police have a good phrase for this: they ruefully talk about new policies being 'doomed to succeed'. You only have to read Margaret Hodge's recent book to see the catalogue of failure.

We work a lot with housing benefits departments. When you give staff the purpose of helping people get back on their feet they do it superbly. Many of the citizens they help end up in tears of relief at having been helped so well – and for the first time in their lives. What we set up could have been the basis for a Universal Credit system that actually worked. It could have been implemented instantly at no cost and with immediate savings with a very willing workforce. When John Seddon explained the opportunity to the minister, he was told that the current system could not be trusted and besides, HMG had already committed to spending the money on the IT. The rest is, and will be, an appalling history.

It becomes apparent that there is no shortage of money, simply vast sums being badly spent. When you fail to do the right thing for citizens you exacerbate their difficulties and need to spend exponentially to resolve it. Given that the subsequent attempts to resolve often don't work either, you have a recipe for unsustainable waste of money and human capital. I spoke to a man who ran a drug rehabilitation unit recently. He said he did what he was asked, ticked all the boxes, made his targets but he had never got a single person off drugs and never will in the current system.

Until recently then, my sense of why managers do not measure against purpose has been the tyranny of targets and regulation which, in turn, stems from the management culture that Deming railed against. But I wasn't happy that it was a fully satisfactory explanation. My revelation came when a colleague showed me a video clip of an interview with Eric Trist. Trist, now dead, had worked with the military during the Second World War helping them to engage the skills and ingenuity of soldiers to design solutions to problems rather than leave 'managers' to impose solutions. it was very successful and Trist, himself a very modest man, felt that many of those problems would never have been solved without that engagement.

After the war Trist worked at the Tavistock Institute and developed an approach called 'socio-technical systems' – how teams of workers can design their own work. It sounds obvious but is still very rare. One of his co-workers was an ex-miner and they were given the opportunity to work in a South Yorkshire pit by a forward-thinking mine manager. That manager had the task of developing a new seam. He was unhappy with the then system which comprised three shifts: shift one worked to break the coal from the seam face, shift two broke the loose coal up and shift three brought it out. The manager's concern was that morale was very low in the work force. Absenteeism was high and men were leaving the pits in significant numbers – an unusual problem for such traditional work.

Trist and his colleague worked with the men to design a new system. The miners decided to operate the same three shift system but with each shift doing all three tasks. Again, it seems obvious and, as you would expect, there was an instant rise in job satisfaction. Absenteeism fell, as did labour turnover. What was also striking was that productivity nearly doubled – it went up over 80%.

In the video, the interviewer asks Trist what the Coal Board did with the experiment. Trist tells him, "They suppressed it"'. When asked why, he cited a number of reasons but the one that registered with me, and Trist speaks it with the tiniest hint of grin, was, "well you need to understand that the job of a mine manager was to be 'in control'".

And there it is. The job of a manager is to be 'in control'. This is what we have taught them: come in on your numbers, make the budget, control your staff.

This logic creates workplaces that are stultifying stress factories. There is no incentive to do a 'good job' merely the necessity to come in on budget, make the numbers and keep the regulators happy. I work in the public sector mostly, these days, and you could be forgiven for thinking that the *de facto* purpose of these organisations is 'be safe'. Safety matters but there is a world of difference between 'be safe' and 'do good things safely'.

The other major criticism of the manager's job as 'controller' is that it stops people learning. There is no incentive to improve and there is no attempt to find out how good things can be. How are we going to thrive in any climate without a system that learns and adapts and wants to be better? We have armies of people across organisations who work in 'improvement' or 'quality' departments, yet they are only required to improve the numbers not the work.

Vanguard is very critical of ISO9000 and in its previous guise of BS5750, the 'quality standard', we took it to task. We asked where the evidence was for the claims it made and it turned out there wasn't any. Our case for this was so clear that the Advertising Standards Agency forced BSI to pull a two-page advert for BS5750 that they placed in the broadsheets.

We did our own research and surveyed 1,000 organisations. 75% said BS5750 had made them worse and 15% reported improvements but when we asked a sample of the 15% none could point to any tangible benefit. We came across a tool maker in the West Midlands who supplied Rover and Honda at the time that the two companies were collaborating. We asked what happened when non-conformities arose. They told us that Rover would come and 'shout at them' and tell them to sort it out. Honda, meanwhile would send their best engineers to help them research the problem and would stay until they had learned how to make the part that Honda needed.

I also worked with a man who had been quality manager at another UK car company. He told me that each vehicle had a number of faults that were 'designed in'. As it came off the production line, every car had to go into a huge pound called 'work in progress'. Isn't it interesting that they couldn't call it 'failure'? Staff came in at weekends to fix them on overtime so at least they were happy. He left the company because he could not get them to understand that it made more sense to 'design the faults out'.

Who has to change it?

So, my thesis is that we all have a significant responsibility to change this. We must start giving managers a better job to do and to do that we must change the stuff we put in their heads. One small part of that is programmes like the MBA. We could start by teaching students how organisations work today so that new managers can be ready to take them on and help them see true purpose and measures.

On the back of the Japanese 'miracle' there was a movement called 'scientific management' – how to use the right data to learn and improve. I am put in mind of Gandhi when asked about Western civilisation. He said, "that sounds like a good idea".

~

Richard Davis works for Vanguard Consulting

About the Editors

Charlotte Pell is Visiting Fellow at Newcastle Business School, Northumbria University and founder of the Little Heresies seminar series. She started her career in local government and it was here she started to follow John Seddon's work. She now works for Vanguard Consulting and her job is to generate curiosity about the Vanguard Method among service managers who want to move beyond command and control management.

Rob Wilson is Professor at Newcastle Business School, Northumbria University with research interests in measurement and performance in public management, co-creation and collaboration of services, data and information sharing in public services and public service reform. His recent work has covered aspects of Digital Economy including innovation in health services and technologies and personalisation of services. He has published widely including the guest editorship of a Special Issue of *Public Money and Management* on Social Impact Bonds and *The Digitalization of Healthcare* and *Digital Government at Work*, both published by Oxford University Press.

Toby Lowe is Senior Lecturer in Public Leadership and Management at Newcastle Business School, Northumbria University. He began academic life as a political philosopher. After completing his PhD he worked in the public and voluntary sectors for 15 years. Before returning to academia he was Chief Executive of Helix Arts, a North East charity specialising in participatory arts practice with marginalised groups. His purpose as an academic is to help improve the funding, commissioning and performance management of social interventions (across the public, private and voluntary sectors).

Jan Myers is Associate Professor in the Newcastle Business School at Northumbria University and co-convenor of the Little Heresies seminar series. Her research interests cover organisational behaviour and HR, and leadership, individual and organisational development in both the UK and Canada, in particular, social entrepreneurship, social capital and mutual organisations with third sector and public sector organisations, both in the UK and internationally.

About the Publisher

Triarchy Press is a small, independent publisher of books that bring a wider, systemic or contextual approach to many different areas of life, including:

The Money System (books by Bernard Lietaer, John Rogers, Margrit Kennedy, Ivo Mosley, Maria Pereira and others)

Government, Education, Health and other public services (books by John Seddon, Richard Davis, Russ Ackoff and others)

Ecology, Sustainability and Regenerative Cultures (books by Daniel Wahl, Nora Bateson and others)

Leading and Managing Organizations (books by Bill Tate, Barry Oshry, Nelisha Wickremasinghe and others)

Walking, Psychogeography and Mythogeography (books by Phil Smith, Alyson Hallett and others)

Movement and Somatics (books by Sandra Reeve, Ernesto Pujol and others)

Innovation (books by Graham Leicester, Andrew Jones and others)

The Future and Future Studies (books by Tricia Lustig, Bill Sharpe and others)

For more information, please visit:

www.triarchypress.net

Lightning Source UK Ltd.
Milton Keynes UK
UKHW020703100620
364730UK00021B/720